I
AM
TESSA

....

TESSA ZIMMERMAN

One Idea Press

Let me tell you a story about an eight-year-old girl who suffered from anxiety. She felt so scared, small and full of panic all of the time. She truly believed that she'd **I** grow up to be a failure, that she would never be normal, that she was bad. Her sobs became wails and her breath **AM** escaped her. She just couldn't stop. She was only eight. Panic attack after panic attack, the little girl felt punished. But she fought through

TESSA

her anxiety, so she could help you overcome.

YOU ARE READING THAT LITTLE GIRL'S BOOK.

by **TESSA ZIMMERMAN**

CONTENTS

"1 in 2 students in the United States expereince anxiety or stress-related behaviors. I was one of those students. What all these children need are the tools and coping mechanisms to thrive. My mission in life is to serve these needs."

In alignment with the mission of this book, a portion of the proceeds of I AM TESSA are donated to ASSET Education, a nonprofit organization that trains teachers in social and emotional tools to help their students mitigate stress and anxiety. In addition, ASSET provides their trained teachers with short lesson plans to make anxiety tools available in everyday classes. Each sale of this book will help ASSET reach its goal of training 200 teachers in New York City and Denver, growing the program to impact more than 20,000 students.

....

HOW TO USE THIS BOOK

I created this book with the intention of it acting as a "tool-box." I've found that there are some books with so many good bits in them that it's helpful to carry them with you. Whenever I felt stressed or anxious, I'd pull out one of those books and dive into one of my favorite pages to help myself feel better.

None of those books, though, were targeted towards young people, and I craved a book that just spoke to my generation.

I wrote this book at nineteen years old, not because I am an expert, but because I know what it's like to be you—I'm right there with you. I also wrote this book to shine a light on the different stakeholders in a teen's life and how they, too, can provide tool-boxes to the teens in their lives.

Yes, that means you guidance counselors, parents, teachers, and social workers...get reading!

My hope is that you will be able to read this book and find tools, techniques, recipes, and mantras that will help you shift from a fearful, stressed, or anxious state into a being who can self-regulate and who knows what it feels like to thrive.

This book is made up of stories from growing up with severe anxiety, tools to cope with anxiety, mantras to swear by, lessons to learn from, and recipes to enjoy. Looking for a tool to calm a panic attack? It's in here! Want to feel better about your body? I've got the recipes to fuel your body and free your mind! Need to shift your perception? The mantras to help facilitate just that are in here.

Use this book as a guide to create your own toolbox. At the very end of the book on page 169, there's actually a section for you to write down which tools you liked best and why. That way, you'll always have the resources you need at the touch of your fingertips. Because, at the end of the day, after reading this book, I want you to know that you can be well, dream big, and panic less.

I'm ready. Are you?

ONE

....

THE REALITY OF GROWING UP WITH ANXIETY

In today's world, we don't share what goes on behind closed doors. We hide behind smiles and phrases like, "I'm fine," when there are so many raw truths under those smiles. We think people won't love us or will label us as "strange" if we really share what's going on in our lives. Well, I never liked being considered normal, so I am peeling back the curtains of my story. I am sharing my raw truths—the painful memories, the most blissful moments, all of it.

According to my parents, I cried the entire first year of my life. I asked my parents if they ever thought something was a little off with me. Their response? "We just hoped you would grow out of it."

I didn't grow out of it. I cried constantly until age thirteen.

Time hop to 2006. I am eleven years old. At eleven years old, my parents and I did not know I had multiple severe anxiety disorders.

We just thought I was absolutely looney tunes.

The school day ends at 2:30pm and my mother is supposed to pick me up because there is no way my anxious body can handle a bus ride with confused, over-achieving middle schoolers who are going through puberty. When the bell rang freedom, I was out of the building, anticipating getting into my mother's car and the rush of relief that would spread through me.

2:31pm and my mother is not there.

Obviously, I think she has abandoned me.

Within a second, full with the fear of abandonment and the idea that I would be stuck at my hell of a middle school, my heart started to beat just a bit faster. The blood pulsing through my veins seemed loud. The world around me simply fell away to where all I could feel was the pain of not being in the safe space of my mother's car.

2:32pm and my mother is still not there.

Pure panic erupts inside of me. There is an aching pain in the back of my throat—a pain associated with knowing I am about to lose all control of myself. I blink faster in an attempt to keep the tears back. I can sense my breath starting to escape me. With all my heart, I do not want to start hyperventilating in the student pick-up line.

2:33pm and there is my mother, in her car, with a smile on her face.

I threw my backpack into the car like I was in the midst of a mad-dash escape from a burning building, and my mother asks me, "How was your day?"

With no strength left to fight my tears and being tired of blinking fast, I start to sob. Not cry. Sob. The day had been filled with countless moments of almost panic attacks.

I think I failed my science test, which really means I probably got 100%. Lunch was a mess because I asked my friends to test me for an upcoming quiz in gym with the flashcards I prepared and they thought that was weird. I just wanted to make sure I knew the difference between aerobic and anaerobic exercise! I am pretty sure it took me twenty tries to open my gym locker, which was quite disastrous as there are only three minutes to change, so I have declared that I will carry my gym clothes with me at all times. That's right, my grocery store plastic bag with my clothes will be attached to me always. I think my so-called friend is hitting me when I am not looking because I haven't been sitting next to her in science class (clearly, I have a reason not to). Today, she gave me a death glare when I passed her in the hallway so I think she is planning to take it up a notch and kill me when I am not looking. These are the thoughts that rack my mind.

My mother just sighs, which makes it worse. I know I have disappointed her. The hopes that I would have a good day is gone. We both know where this is going, and it scares the shit out of us both.

The five-minute drive home is filled with sobs and the phrase, "Tessa, please calm down."

My saint of a mother pulls the car into our driveway, and as she parks, makes an attempt to "start over." I love my mother dearly, but all I want to do is end this nightmare. So instead of listening to her, I run into the house, now shaking and sobbing.

When I enter the safety of my own home, I collapse into a ball on the floor where I start to flail like a fish out of water. I can see my dog, Diesel, from a distance, giving me the "WTF are you doing?" glare. I return his glare and say, "Just casually losing my mind." No sooner does my mother run into the house to find me gasping for air.

Logically, my mother opens all the windows in the house, thinking fresh air will do me some good. But as my gasps and screams get louder, I bang my fists on the floor, begging her to help me stop this insanity. She immediately hurries around, closing all the windows, convinced that our next door neighbors will call the cops or child protective services because I sound like someone is killing me. Except that someone is—my mind is killing me.

This is a Tessa panic attack.

The label "panic attack" sounds incredibly uncomfortable and that's what it is—one of the most uncomfortable experiences a person can have. Yet I know the feeling all too well.

A Tessa panic attack is a recipe of racing thoughts, shallow breath, a touch of hyperventilation, a cup of physical body shaking, and an endless amount of tears.

See, the panic attack starts out small. It can be mitigated, if one knows what they are doing. For me, I know one is starting when I sense a lump in the back of my throat. It hurts. It's present, but it's not quite powerful yet.

The racing thoughts of anxiety will start to speed up and become obsessive. They'll focus on a specific problem like an upcoming test at school and how I feel like I am destined to fail it.

Then, as these racing thoughts become louder and my ability to fight them becomes weaker, tears will run down my cheeks like endless waterfalls. As the tears become heavier and the lump in my throat grows, I start to lose control of my breath. So instead of having a normal-paced breath, mine will speed up, causing my heart to race. My heart feels as if it could burst right through my chest.

The unique element of my panic attacks is that my arms will physically hurt and it feels like there are a million ants under my skin. I do not know why. Maybe it's because it feels like I am having a heart attack.

I wasn't supposed to grow up with panic attacks. I didn't go through any particularly traumatic things in life. I was a normal kid with a somewhat normal family.

I was born to two loving parents who would give me the shirt off their backs time and time again. My father is a Doctor of Oriental Medicine, which is unique, but not in any way traumatic. He's one of the greatest people on this earth as he will do anything in his power to help someone in need. My dad built his practice out of our house so he could be with his daughters. He didn't want to commute and miss out on the opportunity to see my sister and I grow up. This is not the father of a daughter with extreme anxiety—he did nothing to cause or deserve it.

The same goes for my mom, as my dad would say, "Your mommy is the greatest person on the planet." And she is! She is a ballet teacher and Nia instructor. She would try just about anything to make sure her daughter did not suffer—therapy, herbal remedies, blood tests, specific diets. You name it, she made sure I tried it. But it felt as if everything she was trying was hopeless. We couldn't get to the root of it. So she did the little things that kept the attacks at bay, like sleeping beside me when I'd panic myself to sleep.

Then there was my sister, Olivia, who had to grow up with a severely anxious older sister. No one spoke of how Olivia suffered from it, but her life revolved around panic attacks too, and for a long time, she was too young to understand why. Why couldn't her sister fall asleep quietly? Why did she get off the bus to her sister crying over an upcoming test? "Why?" became an endless question for my entire family. We all just couldn't figure out why Tessa was so anxious.

It was frustrating because it felt as if there was nothing we could do to escape my anxiety. We were always managing the anxiety the best we knew how, but there was no amount of love or therapy or specific diets to "cure" my anxiety. It felt as if we were living in a never-ending hell because we just didn't know what might set off a panic attack.

One day, a teacher might look at me "wrong," the next day another student failed their test and it felt as if I had failed too.

The thing about having a child with severe anxiety is that no one talks about how it breaks down a family. Everyone lived on edge because they were afraid to set me off. And worst of all, a lot of people blamed my parents when they did absolutely nothing wrong.

We are all wired differently, and some of us, like myself, are wired to be anxious. In a society driven by results and external accomplishments, an anxious child is left to try and keep up but constantly feels they are just short of being normal. Schools that lack resources to support students individually exacerbate feelings of inadequacy. Our system just isn't built to recognize or support anxious children who need help.

I felt like the burden of my family. But it was my panic attacks that were the burden of my family. And it just plain sucked.

Amongst all the panic attacks, I found perfectionism. It was as if all the anxiety attacks didn't matter as long as I was the perfect student. The 'A' on the paper was a mark that showed I was good at something.

But perfectionism turned into an unhealthy obsession rather quickly.

At eleven years old, I owned a North Face jacket that had a bunch of hidden compartments on the inside of the coat. It's like they created this coat for highly anxious eleven-year-olds who like to bring flashcards with them everywhere. I held hundreds of flashcards on me at any time because you never know when there will be an opportunity to study.

I am dead serious.

I found grocery store trips to be the perfect time to whip out the flashcards and test myself because God forbid if I did not get 100% on everything. There would be hell to pay.

So there I am with my mother in the local grocery store, following her through the aisles, a few steps behind, with my head buried in flashcards.

My mother asks, "Tessa, do you have to study right now?"

And my response, "Mom, do you want me to be a failure in life? Because if I don't get an 'A' on this test, I am destined for nothingness."

With that snarky response, my mother returned to shopping because we both knew there was no way I was giving up being perfect in school. It was the only thing I had.

If my science teacher forgot her notes, she'd use mine. I was that good. And that gave me a sense of pride.

Looking back, I realize the obsession with perfectionism really came from wanting to feel good. When I saw that 'A' on the paper I'd spent hours and hours working on, it felt awesome. My happiness came to depend on my grades.

My happiness was dependent on all external things.

Once I had the 'A,' I had to get another and another. As positive psychologist, Shawn Achor, would say, my goal post was always changing. Because of that, I was unable to experience authentic happiness that actually felt really good.

I thought maybe I'd find this happiness I was searching for on a class trip called Nature's Classroom. The school district sent my sixth-grade class to some outdoorsy program with our teachers. I hoped I'd be able to bond with my fellow peers as that was the point of the trip.

But that whole bonding thing didn't really happen. Let's just say that instead of Nature's Classroom, I think they should have named it Hell.

I had never been away from home for more than a night for a sleepover, and that was plenty for me. However, the bonding experience on this trip was scheduled to go on for an entire three nights and four days. Plenty of time for me to lose my mind.

I boarded the big yellow school bus with a sense of fear overtaking my body. I sat by the window with my face planted on the glass, looking at my mom. She had such a look of hope on her face. I knew she just wanted me to have fun. So I took a deep breath and tried to escape the fear. For once, I just wanted to come back home with a good story, not one filled with panic attacks.

After a two-hour drive, we arrived at the site for Nature's Classroom and it was raining. If the Universe was trying to tell me something, clearly, I was not listening.

We entered our cabins, soaking wet from the rain and relieved to be in a place of shelter. Luckily for me, my cabin mates were my friends. Though they rolled their eyes when I asked them to test me with my flashcards during lunch, we shared laughs and they gave me a sense of community.

Night one and I am hyperventilating in the bottom bunk.

Well, this is embarrassing.

Even worse, the chaperone of my bunk has to ask the guidance counselor to sleep in the bunk next me.

Now I am a certified loser.

I may not be bonding with the other students in my grade, but I sure am getting closer to the guidance counselor.

During the afternoon of the third day, they told us we'd be performing a reenactment of the underground railroad, but first, we must practice the reenactment. Talk about situations way out of your control.

I thought reenacting the underground railroad would be simple. I thought, *It's all fake and they really can't torture us legally, so*

I Am Tessa

I should be okay.

Wrong. I am pretty sure the psychological torture we endured should have been illegal.

During the pre-reenactment, we were squished together to watch some performance where we were yelled at like slaves. When I say squished, I mean we were practically sitting on top of one another. For the anxious eleven-year-old, this is not cool. The sensitive person in me could feel everyone else's fears. It was like my entire grades' emotions were under my skin. I sat there, wanting to erupt, holding back tears. It hurt. I looked at the scared faces around me and I just want to make it better for all of us. We were supposed to find this to be a bonding experience, but I have never felt more alone with the weight of fears upon my chest.

After the pre-reenactment, I ran to my cabin and tried to convince my friends that we should protest this absurd activity. I tried to start a sit-in on my cabin floor, but because of my inability to sleep without a panic attack, my guidance counselor quickly ended the sit-in. So, without even trying, I started to hyperventilate and begged her, in between the gasps, to not make me go. She said it wasn't an option, but she could make sure I was the first group to "escape from slavery."

At that point, all I could do was give in to the insanity that was this Nature's Classroom activity.

I got into my group and we walked into a pitch-black gymnasium where we were to be sold as slaves.

As we entered, I wished I had something to help keep me in

control because the situation was completely out of my control.

Standing in the pitch black, I was completely confused as to what was happening. I could feel the breath of a person behind me on my back, so I sensed I was not alone. All we were told to do is to stand in line and not talk.

Then, I started to hear screaming, not from the students, but from the facilitators of Nature's Classroom. One walked up to me and screamed right into my face, "Your parents are dead. You are worthless. You are nothing but a slave."

With tears in my eyes, I swallowed the pain in the back of my throat. I heard more sobs from other students. I heard the facilitators, screaming:

"I found a good one!"

"If you don't behave, I am going to beat you."

Though I was incredibly scared, all I could think about was how this has to be illegal.

How can they reenact this?

All I felt is that I cannot trust my school. If they put me and all of the other sixth graders through this as a way to bond, there is no way that place is safe. I lost all ability to trust a place of learning because they continued to put me in places of torture.

On average, I spent the majority of my day at school. If I couldn't trust the place I spent most of my time in, how could I expect to learn?

There's an element to our brains called the "fight or flight response." When we feel threatened, our bodies react in such a way that prepares us to handle the worst. Essentially, we are on high alert.

Because I felt that my school was unsafe, I was constantly in fight or flight. I was just waiting for the teacher to give a pop quiz or the bully to say something horrendous. In this waiting stage, I was not focused on learning. I mean, I sat in my classes and took notes, but I wasn't fully present. My eyes darted around the room, making sure no threat was on the horizon. My blood pulsed just a tad bit faster so that every element of my body was ready to respond. It was like being a firefighter, waiting for the next fire to put out, except I was in school, so I should not be waiting for a fire.

I could never just sit in class and take it all in. That'd be way too normal.

It was emotionally exhausting to spend seven hours in a building, pretending I didn't feel like a tiger was about to pounce on my back.

I'd look around in the hallways at the other students and teachers and it made me feel depressed. Everyone looked like they were doing just fine. People were going to their classes, laughing with their friends, planning their next hang outs; but there I was, clenching flashcards and carrying my gym locker clothes with me everywhere.

Something is not right about this picture, I thought, *but I can't let people know how badly I am suffering because then I'd truly be an outcast.*

I tried to keep it together at school. I didn't want to be marked as the loser who cries all the time. I didn't want to be outcasted for something that I had no control over. I feared my peers wouldn't understand what it's like to be afraid to walk out of their own homes every day. Each time I left my home, I felt as if a giant monster might attack me at any moment and swallow me whole. My peers didn't understand, and even worse, neither did my teachers. So, to avoid added frustration and anxiety, I held it all in. I let the monster follow me around every day, just waiting for the moment I got home. That's when everything would erupt and the anxiety, the monster, could swallow me whole.

My parents made a rational decision and arranged a meeting with the school.

They thought that by advocating for their child, in return, they would receive some sort of help. Raising a child with severe anxiety required all-hands on deck, including school teachers and administrators.

The hope was that the school would make some sort of arrangement that would better serve my anxiety or put a support team in place that would make being at school a lot less difficult.

But alas, none of that happened.

See, 'A' students don't really need help. They are getting superior grades, so what's wrong?

Yup, that was the argument for why I didn't need any help—because my grades were so excellent.

What wasn't being seen by the school was that every night I was killing myself studying and suffering with panic attacks just so I could get great grades to make myself look good in the eyes of the school. I just wanted to be normal.

The best the school psychologist could offer was that I should be medicated, and if I were to go to any other school, it wouldn't be better unless I was medicated.

Helpful.

Real helpful.

So, my anxiety continued, and the school made it clear that they would not be providing any additional help unless my parents chose to medicate me.

But my parents and I didn't feel comfortable medicating me at eleven years old.

It just didn't feel right.

Anxiety prevailed, and school officially became the worst place on the planet.

It's midnight on a school night and I am banging my head against the wall.

Typical.

During my anxiety attack, there is a sensation of losing myself. I became very separated from the grounded individual that I knew and loved to being someone that I didn't even recognize. As the panic lasted longer, I started to lose sensation in my body and it became hard to walk or to move any limb because I felt so disconnected.

Amidst this confusion, I discovered it was raining outside. Without even thinking, my body pulled me into the rain. It was as if my brain knew that feeling the rain could help bring me back into my body.

Little did I know, at eleven years old, I was engaging in a mindfulness exercise (maybe a rather extreme one) to help ground myself.

I stood on my concrete driveway with no shoes. I felt the little rocks underneath my feet, and though it was uncomfortable, it felt good because it wasn't anxiety. Then I noticed the rain on my body. Each droplet reminded me that I am a human being with a physical body. I thanked each droplet for reminding me of something I thought I'd lost—my body. I looked up, and as the rain embraced my face and washed away the tear stains, I knew that this was something. For one moment, the anxiety did not seem like it was my entire world. It was just there. The rain helped me simply notice it.

From the outside looking in, this seemed crazy. It was freezing outside and I was wearing just my pajamas with no shoes and standing in the rain.

My parents didn't realize that I was simply practicing mindfulness.

My mother and father begged me to come inside. They stood with an umbrella and with shoes on. They were being normal.

I didn't want to go inside quite yet, but I did. I know this seemed completely irrational to them, and I honor that I did things that scared them, like standing in the rain with no shoes on.

I got under the umbrella, and for the last time, thanked the rain. The rain just gave me relief in a time of crisis.

Though I was frustrated with my parents for disrupting my mindful moment, I felt this strange feeling of gratitude. This strange feeling rippled through my body as if it was the sun waking up the world, and I felt a bit better, a bit more grateful.

Before this moment, I'd thought I had no reason to feel gratitude.

Apparently, sixth grade ended somewhat well enough to give my parents hope that seventh grade would be better.

Except it wasn't. The anxiety got much worse.

My parents had me in therapy, or at least they tried to have me in therapy, but I wasn't really good at the whole thing. Apparently, you cannot be bad at therapy, but I am pretty sure I was. I hated going to therapy with the passion of a thousand suns.

Luckily for me, my dad was good friends with a very well-respected therapist in our town, and with that, the Tessa-therapy initiative began.

The therapist had algae growing in the fish tank in his office. I was a bit obsessive about germs at this time in my life (twelve years old), and the algae made me feel like I was going to get some insane disease just by looking at it.

I know this makes absolutely no sense, but that damn algae had it in for me. I just knew it.

On top of everything else, therapy takes time. It was hour-long conversations about the elements of myself I just didn't feel like talking about.

No, I do not want to talk about how I panicked so badly in class they sent me to the principal's office because I am such a disruption. Therapy was like reliving every moment of anxiety over and over again. Also, I thought I could've been doing significantly more important things during that hour, like studying. I could've been making more flashcards. Or I could've been thinking about all the ways my science teacher might be planning to trick me on my upcoming test on inertia. Therapy just really didn't seem that helpful in the midst of my REAL issues.

So, I just refused to go, because honestly, who could blame me with the homework load I had?

Except my parents were dead-set on the Tessa therapy initiative. Nothing would stop them from making sure I sat next to that algae-infested fish tank for an hour.

Absolutely nothing.

I found myself refusing to go to therapy because I needed to study for an upcoming test, surrounded by flashcards. I had all my textbooks out and I was in the zone—a slightly panicked zone, but I was trying to study.

Then, my dad had some sort of epiphany and figured if he threw my textbooks and flashcards into the back of his car, and made it into the driver's seat just as I dove in to retrieve my things, he could back out of the driveway and I would not know what hit me.

It worked.

I was off to therapy, swimming in tears and flashcards in the backseat of my dad's car. I was also pissed because he really got creative and won that time.

I thought, *This will not fly the next time because over my dead body will I lose another opportunity to study.*

I constantly felt tired. It takes a lot of energy to refuse to go to therapy, suffer from severe anxiety, and go to middle school. I barely got more than a few hours of sleep each night. The only time I could really sleep was between 5am and 7am. My father woke up at 5am, so as soon as I heard him leave my parents' bed, I'd take his place.

I was tired from the endless anxiety. I was having multiple panic attacks during the school day (so much for keeping it together), then would come home just to have more anxiety.

There's a difference between anxiety and panic. Anxiety is the bubbling of fear. Anxiety is this incredibly loud voice that simmers throughout the day, popping up whenever it can. It's the voice in my head that screams, "DON'T BE A FAILURE!" and, "YOU'LL LOOK STUPID IF YOU CRY IN CLASS," or, "YOU DIDN'T STUDY ENOUGH."

A panic attack is when there are no breaks between those comments. They become a constant stream of negativity, invading my mind and taking over my body. A panic attack is the volcano erupting.

My parents were looking into other schools, but I felt I had to take matters into my own hands. I wanted my middle school to know how bad the struggle was to live in this body of mine. I just wanted them to help me, to say, "Tessa, we want to help you."

One Friday morning in seventh grade, I came up with a brilliant plan, or what I thought was a brilliant plan. I was going to tell the guidance counselor (the one who had to sleep in the bunk next to me) that I was going to kill myself. I knew if she could just realize how painful it was to constantly live in fear of losing control, she'd help me. I thought if the school believed I would rather take my own life than continue to live with panic attacks, they would give me tools, resources, more time on tests, anything.

I was wrong, but creative.

So there I am, at about 9am on a Friday morning, and as the words, "I want to kill myself," roll off my tongue, I see the terror in my guidance counselor's eyes.

I think, *Yes, she gets it!* This was the moment I'd been waiting for.

Then she asks, "How are you planning to kill yourself?"

Damnit. I hadn't thought that far in advance.

I searched my mind to come up with a potential way of killing myself.

I blurted out the first thing that came to mind, "With knives. We have sharp knives in my house. You know, for like, cutting steak."

Brilliant. She's sold.

I went on about how hard it is to feel so much fear, day after day. I explained how I couldn't imagine spending the rest of my life like this.

The guidance counselor sent me back to my class, because that's what you are supposed to do when a student tells you they want to kill themselves.

Within thirty minutes, the guidance counselor and vice principal pulled me out of my class to tell me I was going home. They told me this while standing outside my classroom in the hallway, not in a place of privacy! They explained that I was suspended from school until I received a psychiatric evaluation, and that it was unsafe to myself and to my peers to have me in school while I was having such dangerous thoughts. They told me my father was there to take me home.

My heart sank into my stomach. That was not what I wanted. I'd just asked them to help me, to just please give me resources, tools, anything, but not this. *Don't kick me out so you don't have to deal with it.*

I met my father at the school entrance with a very heavy heart. I didn't want this for him or my mother or my sister. I could see in his face how sad he was.

As we walked out of the building, I tried to explain to my father how I hadn't meant for this to happen. I told him how all I wanted to do was to get the school to help me. I wanted them to know how painful it was to live in my body, and how I thought if they knew I wanted to kill myself, they would help me. I never thought they would suspend me from school. But I guess I was wrong.

I arrived home and curled up in a ball on the couch. *Now, I feel like I actually want to kill myself.* My only hopeful plan had completely backfired into getting me suspended from school. The pain in the back of throat left me feeling raw. I was too depressed to even have an anxiety attack, but relieved to not be in that dreadful place called school.

I hadn't even been home for thirty minutes when the house phone rang.

It was my fourth grade teacher, Mrs. I. At that point, Mrs. I was the only educator who had really taken the time to understand me and push me past my anxiety. This anxious fourth grader was actually class president in her room, where I learned leaders don't cry every time they have to do math (that was a concept that took me a while to grasp). She taught me tools to calm me down and let me bring things that comforted me when I had to take tests.

I've kept in touch with Mrs. I since the fourth grade. She knew that I was having an extremely difficult time in middle school and checked in on me whenever she could.

My father answered the phone, and with a huge smile on his face, said to Mrs. I, "Your timing is impeccable!"

I curled up into a tighter ball because if there is one person who could actually make me feel like I could push through it, it was Mrs. I. But I didn't have her to be tough on me or to be my cheerleader when I needed one in middle school. I was alone there.

My dad explained the entire situation to Mrs. I. Then she wanted to speak to me.

Oh, no. Here it comes.

Mrs. I told me that we would be getting breakfast together the next morning. She told me she loves me and to be strong. I held back tears of relief. I think it's extremely special when a teacher tells you she loves you and will let you come to her house at 8am on a Saturday to give you a pep talk. I may not have gotten the school to help me, but at least one educator in my life was willing to be there for me.

The next day, I woke up excited to see Mrs. I. Though these were not the best circumstances, the chance to spend time with her and her cute two-year-old daughter was worth it. I walked into her house and she gave me the biggest embrace. I knew I was safe.

We chatted for a few hours, but these words hit me in the heart.

"What's going to happen to the rest of us of who love you if you commit suicide? How are we going to feel?"

I was sitting next to a woman whom I greatly admired, who made me feel like I actually mattered, even though I had all kinds of anxiety and difficulty functioning. People cared about me and wanted me to live beyond these limits. My middle school may not have cared much about me, but I realized then that my family and Mrs. I did, and that was enough.

My suspension from school lifted with a note from a family friend who is a psychiatrist which basically stated I was mentally sane enough to enter the school building.

My guidance counselor made me a contract to sign stating that I would not kill myself in school, and she gave me a stress ball for when times get tough. Apparently, a stress ball can prevent you from killing yourself, at least while in school.

I started to get the hint that the school really didn't care about my mental wellbeing, and I accepted that.

The following week, I came home from school, and in my usual routine, I played the voicemails left on my home phone.

That's when I heard the words, "Hi, this is Holly, the guidance counselor from Coley Middle School. After some observation since Tessa has been back in school, we are concerned that your daughter might be struggling more than we anticipated. For further support, we'd like to suggest you take Tessa to Hallbrook for further clinical evaluation. Please contact my office with any questions."

Hallbrook is our town's psychiatric hospital.

First off, who thinks it's a good idea to leave a voicemail telling a student's parents that they should take their child to the local mental hospital?

When I heard these words, my heart sank into the pit of my stomach. *I know I may not be perfect and I may lose control of my body, but I am not going to be stuck in a mental hospital. That is not where I belong.*

I told myself that I would not let that happen. With all my heart, I refused to be cast off into a local mental hospital at twelve years old because my particular middle school didn't want to deal with me.

After that voicemail, the search for a scholarship to go to a private school began. My parents and I could no longer be hopeless. Somewhere inside of us, we knew I could thrive somewhere else. We didn't know where or how, but we had hope that I could get out of my current middle school and find a place that would teach me how to cope with anxiety.

I will feel normal and I will live a life beyond my wildest dreams.

THE FOUNDATIONAL TOOLS

Throughout my childhood, I spent a lot of time desperately looking for someone to help me with my anxiety. It was difficult to know who to talk to, what to do, or how to handle what was happening to me. Do you feel confused about where to start your journey to feeling better and less anxious? Don't panic! To help you, I've assembled this group of basic tools, not overly complicated and simple to implement. Pick one to start with today. Why right now? You know you'll tell yourself, "I'll try this later," and then you never actually do because life gets in the way and it's easy to do what's comfortable. So start with #1 and see if it resonates with you. Not every tool fits everyone, so try them all out. Some might feel great and others might not. That's okay! The goal is to build your toolbox, so find the ones that best resonate with you.

Don't forget! In the back of the book, there's a section where you can document which tools you like best and what pages they are on. This way, you can more clearly craft your toolbox by jotting down which tools you enjoyed.

#1 Meditation
REVISED GARBAGE TRUCK MEDITATION

I learned the Garbage Truck Meditation from an article on how meditation can help calm anxiety. It was called the Garbage Truck for its ability to clear yucky thoughts out of one's head, but I thought I'd give it some Tessa spice, thus we have the Revised Garbage Truck Meditation to help clear the junk out of your head.

Find a quiet spot, maybe it's your bed or a local park, or if you're me, it's your closet. (I'm not kidding. I like to sit in my closet, close the door, and meditate.) No matter how strange it may seem to the outside world, find your place of peace; do what is best for you.

Once you are there, discover the position that is most comfortable for you. It might be laying down or sitting upright with pillows supporting your back, or simply wrapping yourself in blankets. Create this special space for you.

Now that you feel most comfortable, close your eyes and check-in. Scan your body for any tension. Remove your tongue from the roof your mouth. Move your jaw a few times. Add in some neck rolls. Really get a sense of where you are at. After you've checked in with your body, you can begin. Say the following phrase six times, each for a minute, and at different noise levels.

The phrase is, "Peace belongs to me." As you say, "peace," touch your thumb to your pointer finger. As you say, "belongs," touch your thumb to your middle finger. As you say, "to," touch your thumb to your ring finger. As you say, "me," touch your thumb to your pinky finger. Repeat these actions as you say the phrase. Now, for the different noise levels. Below are the noise levels for which you should say the phrase for each minute.

1. Whisper

2. Loud

3. In your head

4. In your head

5. Whisper

6. Loud

You'll repeat the phrase as many times as you can throughout each minute at each noise level while doing the action of touching your thumb to each finger. Remember, this may seem awkward at first, but don't get too caught up in how ridiculous this is and just enjoy the experience.

After you've completed six minutes of clearing the junk out of your head, sit with yourself and just notice how you feel. When you feel ready, go back to your day. Know that this meditation is here for you at any point when you need to release negative thoughts.

#2 Mantra

WHEN I FEEL IMPERFECT, I REMIND MYSELF THAT I AM WHO I AM AND THAT IS PURE PERFECTION.

The reason I chased perfectionism was because I didn't know who I was and how to cultivate happiness within myself. I thought I was perfect, which was Tessa. But see, Tessa wasn't perfect. Tessa was Tessa and that is what made me perfect and ultimately happy because I didn't have to hide behind a persona I thought I was.

#3 Recipe
CALM YOURSELF SMOOTHIE

This smoothie is ultimately the best for colds, but there is something about liquefied greens that just soothes my soul. I can be feeling like an absolute mess and my anxiety can be radiating around me, but if I wash down a huge glass of greens, I feel the tension in my body release. You don't need to have a cold or tons of anxiety to drink your greens, but if you're experiencing either, I HIGHLY recommend going green.

Ingredients:

2 kale leaves

2 collard leaves

½ cucumber

1 pear

¼ inch of ginger

1 garlic clove (optional)

1 glass of water, filled to the top

Instructions:

1. Place all the fruits and veggies in the blender.
2. Pour water over the fruits and veggies.
3. Blend until smooth.

#4 Recipe
GROUNDING BUTTERNUT SQUASH SOUP

Who doesn't love a soup recipe that makes you feel whole from the inside-out? This was a recipe shared with me by my mindfulness teacher, Miss Casey, who taught me the healing power of food. This is one of my favorite dishes for lunch!

Ingredients:

1.5 pounds butternut squash

1 large sweet potato

Bone broth (I use Pacific's Organic Turkey Bone Broth)

Coconut milk

Salt

Pepper

1 tablespoon cinnamon

Equipment:

Blender/food processor

Small pot

Instructions:

1. Pre-heat oven to 400°F.

2. Wash butternut squash and put in oven.

3. After cooking butternut squash for 15 minutes, put the washed sweet potato in the oven.

4. Cook the butternut squash and sweet potato for 45 more minutes.

5. Take out of the oven and scoop the inside of the butternut squash (except the seeds) and sweet potato out and into your blender/food processor.

6. Once the sweet potato and butternut squash are in the food processor, pour the bone broth in until it fills up ¾ of the surrounding area around the butternut squash/ sweet potato.

7. The remaining ¼ area should be filled with the coconut milk. There should not be more liquid than there is squash and potato.

8. Add 1 tablespoon of cinnamon and salt and pepper, to taste.

9. Blend away until soup is evenly mixed and puréed.

10. Pour into pot and heat on stove on a medium-low setting.

11. Enjoy! This recipe serves two, so share it with a friend.

#5 Tool
MINDFULNESS

In the story of my anxiety attack in the rain, I shared how the gift of rain and the sensation of droplets on my body helped calm me down. Little did I know, I was practicing mindfulness in that very moment. The conscious choice to watch the rain on my body instead of focusing on the anxiety in my head was an act of mindfulness.

Mindfulness is all about watching the thoughts in your mind or sensations in your body without judgement. Though I did judge how weird it must have looked to my parents to have their daughter standing in the pouring rain, I didn't focus on it for too long.

A simple way to practice mindfulness is to find a quiet place (just like we did in the Garbage Truck Meditation) and watch your breath. I like to notice the sensation of my chest rising and falling. If a thought comes up, I simply notice it. As the Strala yoga guru and founder, Tara Stiles, would say, "If a thought is important enough, it will come back to you."

I challenge you to take two minutes to notice the sensation of your chest rising and falling. When a thought pops up in your head (because we are humans and we like to think), just let it dance away and return your awareness to the sensation of your breath. Each day, add another minute to your mindfulness breath time. See if you can get up to ten minutes.

Take notice of how being mindful affects your life. Are you a little less obsessed with the thoughts in your head and a little more present in this big, grand experience called life? Or maybe you're simply mindful of how jittery you get when you drink a cup of coffee? It can be big or small, and either way, it's an important shift.

#6 *Lesson*
ASK FOR HELP

I shared my suicide announcement story not to criticize how the school handled my anxiety, but to shed light on the concept of asking for help. Human beings naturally want to help each other.

What I failed to do was ask for help in a concise way. Instead, I told the school something I thought would get them to help me, but I didn't directly ask for help.

The better way to have gone about this would have been to clearly state the problem and where I was struggling. I didn't ask for resources or tools to help me, nor did I ask if the school could do anything on their end to provide support. Who knows how they would have responded, but I do know I wouldn't have gotten suspended for asking.

When we state how we are feeling and what we need, people will respond in ways that will surprise us. The challenge may be figuring out who you can ask for help from. Start with your family, school guidance counselors, therapists, or teachers. Find someone who you can trust and is capable of helping you. If you tell a friend about what you're struggling with and ask for help, they may not be in a position to provide the resources you need—not because they are a bad friend, but because they just don't have enough experience in this area.

Don't be afraid to ask for help. We are human, which means we require help at some points during our lives.

#7 Mantra
I CHOOSE NOT TO LIVE IN OTHER PEOPLE'S FEARS.

This is absolutely one of my favorite mantras. When the guidance counselor left the voicemail telling my parents to take me to the local mental hospital, I made a choice not to let her fear of my anxiety be my own fear. There are many times where we might be fearful of something and we may not understand why, but it might be because we are taking on other's fears as our own.

People often project their fears onto us (especially when we are young), and it's easy to adopt those fears as our own. The key to recognizing fear projection is to ask yourself, "Is this my own fear? Where is this coming from?"

Once you've identified whether a fear is someone else's or your own, you'll find relief in knowing the root of the issue. This is where the mantra comes in to help you re-affirm this new identification.

When you recognize a fear that is not your own, take action by stating this mantra.

TWO

....

TAKING RISKS LEADS TO DREAMING BIG

The time came when I was offered to attend a private school, Easton Country Day School, on a full scholarship. A family friend of ours had been sending her children to a school fifteen minutes away from where we lived and she swore it was the right place for me. After months of searching, the opportunity was right in front of me. I could taste the chance for a fresh start, but it wasn't that easy.

My repeat negative experiences at my middle school left me traumatized. I associated school with words like fear and mistrust. School was not a loving or learning place. In my eyes, it was purely unsafe.

I sat on my parents' bed with "thank you" notes spread across the covers. These "thank you" notes were for the teachers—the ones who really didn't care much about my anxiety at all. I almost felt like writing, "Thank you for putting up with me."

My mother could see in my eyes that I was afraid of the risk that I was taking. She looked at me and said, "You know, you don't have to go. We can figure something out. You've been with the same group of peers since kindergarten. It's understandable if you want to stay."

She was right. It would've been easier to stay at my hellish middle school. It would've been easier to not have to make a new group of friends at a new school. It would've been easier to stay with what I know. But in my heart, there was something wrong with staying.

I knew if I stayed, nothing would change. I had to be thrown completely out of my comfort zone in an attempt to have a real life with less anxiety.

So I told my mom, "I am going to my new school."

Those words frightened me, but at the same time, I was proud to say them because they meant that I was making a different choice—a choice to help myself.

By my second day of eighth grade, I was convinced that I was not walking into my new school. I sank my weight into the passenger seat of my mother's car and tucked my chin so she couldn't see the tears rolling down my face.

"I can't go," I said to her.

My mother responded, "What do you mean you can't go? It's your second day at this school."

"I can't," is all I could muster.

"I am going to get Mrs. Inwood," my mother declared as she got out of the car.

Every curse word in the English language went off in my head. How can she be getting the principal of the school on the second day? I was already starting off the school year by getting in trouble.

Then I started to sob because it had taken so much courage to get in the car and sit quietly while my mother drove the fifteen minutes to school. As I stared at the entrance, all that courage was gone, and pure fear erupted inside of me.

As I sat and waited, I remembered the time my English teacher shook my binder to make sure no papers fell out. Or the time my science teacher asked me for my notes because she'd forgotten hers. Or that so-called "friend" who would hit me when I wasn't looking. Suddenly, every panic attack I'd had in a school setting flashed before my eyes, scaring me enough to actually panic.

I started to lose my breath. I gasped desperately trying to get air into my lungs. I wrapped into a tiny ball and rocked back and forth in the seat, trying to calm myself down.

When I saw my mother and my new principal come walking, the epic list of curse words returned to my mind.

They were walking toward me and all I could think was, "Remain normal." I wiped the tears from my eyes and swallowed back the pain in my throat. I refused to hyperventilate in front of my new principal. *Mrs. Inwood will not see me like this.*

Once my mother and Mrs. Inwood reached the car, the scariest possible thing happened. My mother went on a walk while Mrs. Inwood sat in the driver's seat of my car next to me.

RED ALERT. RED ALERT. RED ALERT.

I was in some deep trouble. My eyes widened and my eyebrows raised to almost meet halfway up my forehead. I could feel the shocking expression on my face. I sat absolutely frozen in my seat, trying to muffle the sounds of my cries.

The first words out of Mrs. Inwood's mouth were, "Hi, honey."

Honey? Is she referring to me as honey? Does this mean I am not in trouble?

Then she continued, "What do you feel right now?"

She didn't say, "Are you okay?" This was totally new. Before I could even answer, I had to get out of my sense of confusion. Everyone always assumes I am not okay, but she was okay with wherever I was at.

"I don't want to go in. It's unsafe."

"You know, you are safe with me, and I make sure that school is a completely safe place. No one is going to hurt you here. I know this is scary, but you have to trust me."

Trust? You? I barely know you. The only educator I've ever trusted in my life before this is Mrs. I.

"I don't know."

I don't know how to trust someone.

Then Mrs. Inwood did this strange thing. She hugged me. She wrapped her arms around me, and in that moment, I knew I could trust her. I gained this understanding that she got it and she wasn't afraid of me or my anxiety. I was not a threat to her school, and in her eyes, I was actually an asset. I was not this anxious student she has no idea how to deal with. In fact, she actually did know how to deal with my anxiety.

In that moment, I felt safe.

"You do not have to go to classes. In fact, all I ask is that you sit and read in my office next to my desk until noon. Then you can go home."

"Okay...does it look like I've been crying?" I wiped the tears from eyes and tried to smile.

"No. You're fine, honey."

We got out of the car and walked into the building together where I spent the next four hours beside Mrs. Inwood's desk with my head in a Jodi Picoult novel. I did not take off my coat as I refused to make myself feel like I was staying long. And though I counted down the hours, it was the first time in a long time that I didn't actually have an anxiety attack in a school building.

Mrs. Inwood quickly became my lifeline, my person who understood my anxiety and had the power to alter school in such a way that enabled me to attend.

In addition to Mrs. Inwood and her support, it became clear I needed more people in my corner, a.k.a. a therapist I was willing to talk to.

Dirty fish tank therapist was not cutting it.

Trying on therapists is like trying on shoes. Some look damn good, but are rather uncomfortable to wear. Some look questionable, but fit great.

The hunt for the perfect therapist was on, and it wasn't always pretty.

I was trying on therapist #5...who really knows at this point? In the middle of our conversation, #5 says, "I think you're going to live at home for the rest of your life and not attend college."

Well, um, was that supposed to be insightful? Because it certainly isn't helpful.

My eyes got wide and I couldn't take it anymore.

I was tired of being told what I couldn't do because of the wiring of my brain. I was so tired of being outcasted as a failure. But I was even more tired of telling my parents that this therapist wasn't a right fit either. I couldn't even bring myself to tell them why.

"Well, this one thought I was going to live at home with you guys forever, so I would say this one isn't the right therapist."

I could just see my parents trying to hold back tears and be strong.

It wasn't worth telling them.

So it was Mrs. Inwood and I who would take on the world—my lifeline and I.

In being my lifeline, I constantly sent Mrs. Inwood emails. The fear of school the next day was so intense for me that I had to know what our plans were. Mrs. Inwood and I would take each day one at a time, figuring out what I could handle and what needed to be eliminated (which usually was homework).

To give you a glimpse into my anxious life, I thought I'd share these emails from the "early days" of Tessa.

October 14, 2009

Hi Mrs. Inwood,

I am extremely worried about school. Every time I think about going, I feel a sense of panic. I am unsure....(Tessa was unable to finish this email because her emotions got the best of her.) Best, Jeff

January 30, 2010

Hi Mrs. Inwood,

I crashed and burned very badly. I haven't gotten out of the house or out of bed for that matter. I feel so anxious that I have made myself sick! I don't know what to do! Love, Tessa

February 22, 2010

Hi Mrs. Inwood,

I am extremely anxious. I cannot stop worrying about school! I really want to be home schooled! My parents are very upset because I am barely eating and won't let me workout. I am really miserable and can't function! I don't know what to do! Love, Tessa

The most amazing part? Mrs. Inwood responded to every single email I ever sent with love, patience, and gratitude. The early days might have been extremely challenging with having trouble functioning and getting out of the house, but it was Mrs. Inwood and her consistent responses and love that made it possible.

As eighth grade ended, we figured it was time I spend a larger part of the day in the classroom rather than hiding from the world in Mrs. Inwood's office.

But I didn't give up on the search for a therapist. In fact, I become more determined to find someone who would tell me that I could go to college and live away from home if I put in the work.

Finally, we found Todd, who didn't show disappointment in my anxiety. Todd was a dad and got that kids wanted to overcome their obstacles. He believed they could.

At this time, I felt a little more open to therapy. Maybe it was because I was older or maybe because Mrs. Inwood wasn't allowing me to take tests so I didn't have to worry about studying. Either way, I liked talking about all the crazy anxiety because it felt good to get it off my chest. Though I was reliving it, I was also releasing it.

I also really enjoyed making my parents happy by going to therapy. I got to be a daughter they could feel proud of when I entered Todd's office because I was making a decision that was beneficial to me.

Yup, that may seem weird. Proud that their daughter goes to

therapy? That's not typical in society and often, looked down upon. But let me tell you, therapy can be the absolute best. I mean, I get to talk about all the crazy, wacky anxiety in my brain and not be judged!

Absolutely rad.

My mom was grateful to have Mrs. Inwood and Todd's guidance because it gave her tools as a parent. Taking action steps as a team and having two coaches that we could work with as a family made living with anxiety a little less harsh and a little more possible.

I was a proud therapy-attender now and I think it was because I could understand its importance in kicking anxiety's butt.

As I entered my second year at ECDS, I learned I would have a bodyguard.

You know you are cool when you are in ninth grade and have been assigned a bodyguard. Or, you're officially a loser who is having trouble getting into the classroom without having a massive panic attack.

I looked across the table at my bodyguard and immediately, I can tell he's an introvert too. That he gets me.

As my new bodyguard, Nathan, sat on his computer while I read my book, I casually peered up and looked at him, but when we made eye contact, I moved the book in front of my eyes. This continued for an hour, until we tried to go to class.

I entered my classroom with a new sense of confidence because

I knew if I had an anxiety attack, I had an escape plan. The hardest part about going to class was the feeling of being trapped in the room if something were to go wrong, like if I had a panic attack. With Nathan there to be my out, it wasn't so bad.

We were in biology class and something did not make sense. I couldn't keep up with the teacher and I couldn't communicate that I didn't understand. So, I sat there, with the pain in the back of my throat killing me.

I whispered to Nathan, "I need to go."

Without even asking why, Nathan and I left the classroom.

In the hallway, tears started to pour down my face while Nathan searched for an empty room to protect me from the students that were about to rush through the hallway. I could feel the adrenaline pulsing through my veins as I obsessed over not being able to understand my biology class.

Finally, Nathan found a room, just in time, before the herds of students erupted into the hallway. I curled into the tiniest of balls, and then Nathan taught me one way to calm myself. Receiving hugs provided sensory input. For me, that's being squeezed. Nathan conducted some occupational therapy by squeezing my arms and giving me a really tight hug.

Damn, my bodyguard gets it. Hallelujah!

I've learned that the people you need in your life only show up when you're ready for them. Thus, my support group, known as "my tribe," showed up in layers, each new layer appearing when I was able to learn from them.

First off, my parents were not in my tribe (not that I don't love them). But my tribe was a designated group of people I could go to for different reasons, who would provide their own unique support style. I was stuck with my parents, but my tribe was my own group who I had carefully selected, or I should say, had been carefully selected for me by some higher power.

The first person in the Tessa Tribe was Mrs. Inwood, of course. She was the one to give me a full scholarship to her school. The one who let me sit in her office and read for six months as my form of schooling. She never once doubted my ability to function as a human being, and thus, never let me give up. It didn't matter if I was hiding in my bed, the car, a corner of a room—she would find me and bring me to school. I was allowed to email or call Mrs. Inwood any time of the day. For that, she was the first member of my tribe.

Next came Jamie, Mrs. Inwood's daughter, who, like me, struggled significantly with anxiety growing up. Now, she was in graduate school at Yale. Jamie was my first anxiety role model. Jamie was brilliant, funny, graceful, yet living with anxiety ALL AT THE SAME TIME. She met with me every Sunday at Barnes & Noble where we'd sit in the cafe and learn about how to do school related activities the anxiety way. I learned about how important it was to write things down that had to be done instead of letting them boil up in my head, only to later explode into an anxiety attack. It was Jamie's graceful and quirky approaches to anxiety that earned her a spot in the Tessa Tribe.

Nathan, the bodyguard, was the third member of my tribe for his unique ability to swiftly rescue me from disastrous panic attacks in the classroom. Nathan's presence allowed me to challenge myself and stay in the classroom, even when I wanted to escape. With Nathan there, I began to push beyond my limits and challenge the anxiety. In my high school graduation speech, I referred to Nathan as my backbone, because he was just that. For the times when I didn't have any strength to show up to class, I still did, but with my external backbone by my side.

In tenth grade, I was blessed with two new members of my tribe, Mr. Quirk and Miss Casey. Both walked into my life just as I needed them to. Mr. Quirk took over as the high school director and instantly was a tribe member. He made fun of my anxiety just as much (or more) than Mrs. Inwood did and was my person who could laugh at my ridiculousness with me whenever. But honestly, what earned him his brownie points was that whatever crazy dream I had, he joined in on it with all his heart. He pushed me to follow ideas I had and to test different potential careers, like the time I wanted to be a child neuropsychologist and he gave me a project to study three-year-olds. With Mr. Quirk in my corner, the world became limitless.

Arriving with Mr. Quirk was my sweet Miss Casey who, too, became an anxiety role model. Miss Casey was my mindfulness teacher, and before then, I had not been ready to have her show up in life. She came at a time when I was ready to look at myself and my thoughts without judgement and to make conscious shifts. Within Miss Casey's presence, I could tell I breathed a bit easier and my mind raced just a tad less. She became not only my big sister, but one of my best friends, and thus, a tribe member.

This tribe of mine formed over a few years and will forever be part of me. I may not see them every day or chat with them every week, but within their presence, I feel incredibly safe, loved, and supported.

THE COURAGEOUS TOOLS

Life requires courage. There will always be moments that scare us in the best possible way. It's the moments we feel like we're jumping off a cliff into an enormous black abyss when, in actuality, we're just deciding which college we should to go to. Or, the time we ask that person out who we've been meaning to ask out, even when it just seems too embarrassing or way too risky. Maybe it's the day you decide you're not going to choose the path of your parents and instead, make a path of your own. These moments are not meant to paralyze us, but remind us of how courageous we truly are. But when these situations seem a bit too overwhelming, these tools are there to have your back.

Make sure you write down the ones that work best for you in your own toolbox section on page 169.

#8 Mantra
I OWN MY COURAGE.

I've come to the conclusion that life is about consciously owning your courage and moving in the direction that constantly challenges this courage of yours. I tell the story of sitting on my mother's bed because it was the first time I identified with being courageous. Don't get me wrong, looking back on life, I have been nothing but courageous, time and time again. But it was this moment that I consciously chose courage.

This mantra is to help in the moments when you need courage. In the moments that scare the absolute shit out of you, I ask that you make a choice to own your courage, and to tell yourself that as many times as it takes for you to believe it.

#9 Tool
YOGA

First off, I am not a yoga teacher, but I am a hot yoga junkie, and when I can't leave my apartment, I am practicing Tara Stiles yoga sequences on YouTube. For a while, I felt afraid and uncomfortable practicing yoga in front of people. (I'd like to blame my middle school gym class for my fear of looking "stupid" or "awkward" when doing any form of movement in front of others.) So, for a long time, YouTube yoga was my go-to!

When my anxiety is high, I do not feel present in my body. It's as if my mind is taking over the entire show. Yoga brings me back into my body. I practiced Tara Stiles yoga videos and discovered that all the anxious thoughts would dissipate and I would once again be Tessa, not anxious Tessa. The physical practice of moving with my breath and not moving from a place of tension is how my sensory system finds itself again.

If I've had a panic attack the night before, I make sure to roll out my yoga mat in the morning. It might take me twenty minutes to get out of bed, but when I settle into Child's Pose on my mat, it's as if I am home again.

I may not be able to carry my yoga mat with me everywhere I go for when panic arises, but I can bring the practice with me. That might mean practicing a handstand against a tree or simply connecting my breath to each step I take as I walk. I do know that when I make time for a class or to practice a sequence at home, the magnitude of anxiety I feel diminishes.

Yoga helps me recognize how strong my body is and how much courage I really do have.

#10 Mantra

WHEN I COMMUNICATE MY FEELINGS AND NEEDS, I AM SUPPORTED.

When one asks, one receives. It's a fairly simple concept, but it takes one thing—trust. In middle school, though I was able to communicate my feelings sometimes (usually rather dramatically), I never trusted that I would receive the help I needed. I didn't believe I would receive support, and thus, I never did.

I absolutely love this mantra because when I practice it enough, every part of my being believes that I am supported in what I need. Even when I am having bad anxiety, I make sure to tell those around me that I am, and usually the Universe steps in and those people help to lift me up. All I ask is that when you practice this mantra, you surrender and trust. Discover what surrendering and trusting means to you.

#11 Tool
HOW TO CREATE YOUR OWN TRIBE

Building your tribe is rather important. These are the people who just simply "get" you, there's no trying or faking it. They may be your mentors, educators, friends, relatives, whomever, but these people are sacred to you and your growth.

I am currently in the process of building my Boulder, Colorado tribe. I have my people back in Connecticut where I am from, but living in Boulder by myself with no family has been a challenge. What I've learned from this tribe building process is to not get caught up in it. So what if you only have one person who you can talk to, or maybe no one! I started in Boulder with NO ONE and made it work. But it takes patience and gratitude for the people that are in your life.

I also spend time going to places where I might find a potential tribe member, whether it's hitting up the yoga studio every day and seeing the people who normally take the same classes as you, or going to events where people of like minds may be. One must take risks to find their tribe.

You may also start building your tribe by looking for a therapist or by finding a meditation class. Again, one must reach out to build their tribe, but also trust that the right people and friendships will form as you are ready for them.

#12 Mantra

HOW I LOVE MYSELF SETS THE STANDARD FOR HOW OTHERS WILL TREAT ME.

Tribe Building 101: One must love themselves in order to have people around them who will love them as well. This is simple, friends. Start finding the little things within yourself that you love and are grateful for. Maybe it's your sense of humor or maybe you make a kick-ass smoothie, but whatever it is, start to find what you appreciate about yourself and then practice this mantra, setting the intention that by honoring yourself, others will honor you as well.

THREE

....

BECOMING THE CRAZY KALE LADY (AND LOVIN' IT)

I was diagnosed with Lyme disease within my first year at Easton Country Day School. I remember telling my fellow class-mates, who I sometimes went to class with when I felt sick of Mrs. Inwood's office or when I felt I should expand my friendships past just my bodyguard.

The first question I was asked: "It's not like cancer, right? You're not going to die, right?"

Lyme disease is not something you die from, but for some rea-son, I found it cool that I had a disease. I had not been officially diagnosed with my multiple anxiety disorders yet, so having a disease seemed pretty neat and special.

The mind of a thirteen-year-old is rather strange.

With my diagnosis came a heavy dose of antibiotics, which left me feeling like crap and unable to hold food down. My diet con-sisted of plain pasta, bananas, applesauce, and toast, which also made me feel like crap.

The bonus of not being able to hold any food down? Losing weight.

At a time when everyone was obsessed with their body, I loved my new sick body. I was ninety-five pounds, thin and cute. I didn't have to exercise. My high dosage of antibiotics did all the work for me.

Losing fifteen pounds in a short period of time left me obsessed with my body. I wanted it to stay small and cute. Thus, the brilliant conclusion was to stop eating.

Lack of food + antibiotics = thin & cute, right?

But really, it was more like:

Lack of food + antibiotics = thin, irritable, anxious & obsessive

Not only did I refuse to eat for 36-48 hours at a time, but I used it as a weapon and leverage against my parents.

I became angry at my parents for not taking me out of middle school earlier. I felt the extra trauma I had endured was their fault. In my eyes, they hadn't fought hard enough for me.

Now that I had a taste of the good school life, one where the director of the school cared about me and helped me push through my anxiety, I was mad that I hadn't had that earlier, and instead, had to work through even more built up trauma.

So I used the lack of food consumption to upset them. I knew it hurt them when I starved myself for hours on end, and it thrilled me. Not only did I have control over my body being thin, but I had control over how I made my parents feel.

School wasn't contributing to my anxiety in the same way it had in the past. My obsession over my body began because my anxiety needed to attach itself to something else. Focusing on my body in a search to gain control gave my anxiety new fuel.

Anxiety is silent to the outside world, but very loud to the person who is experiencing it. I had to make sure everyone around me (at least in my family) knew how bad the internal experience was for me.

What a powerful weapon.

I didn't know how to express all the anxiety and anger I felt other than having panic attacks and refusing to eat.

I ended up denying myself nutrients and the energy my body needed to heal my anxiety as well as my Lyme disease, which was unfortunate. I also failed to communicate my feelings with my parents, and instead, chose actions that caused them worry.

Little did I know, I would learn the lesson of how I was hurting myself, not just my parents, from an incident with Navy SEAL candidates.

I knew my dad had been working with Navy SEAL candidates and teaching them energy medicine, but what I did not expect was to arrive home one night to six of them working out in my house.

My parents converted our garage into a dance studio years before for my mother to teach private dance lessons and for my father to practice his martial arts. Now it was being used as a workout space for the candidates.

I walked into my house, carrying a bunch of Indian food to the words, "HOORAH!" I almost jumped with surprise.

What are they doing in there?

Of course, I had taken gym in school before, but I never really cared for it, nor did it actually feel like a workout. It felt more like mental torture and embarrassment than an actual physical workout.

So, as I saw these Navy SEAL candidates completing hundreds of push-ups and burpees as they said phrases like, "It's all mind over matter. if I don't mind it, then it doesn't matter," I became fascinated.

I had never really resonated with exercise at all. I always felt embarrassed while doing any physical activity. But as I saw these six Navy Seal candidates pushing their bodies to their absolute limits, where some were even puking, it made me believe that exercise may be a key ingredient to the recipe of living with anxiety.

I'd like to blame gym class for making me feel like exercise was not my thing. I wasn't the athletic type. I have absolutely no hand-eye coordination. I was always picked last for the sports teams. I hated changing for gym class, mostly because I could never open my locker, but also because I didn't feel comfortable in my body. I never understood why we had gym class other than it was a legal requirement? On top of that, they gave tests in gym class. I mean, who does that?

Then I saw these Navy SEAL candidates training for a job that was dangerous. If they got into the Navy, they'd be the best of the best. I watched them with such fascination because I couldn't understand how they were doing a hundred push-ups and then what seemed like a billion sit-ups, and then more. They would always push through more. Their bodies would be in excruciating pain, but they'd fight to accomplish more.

I came to really admire that element of pushing through despite how one may feel. They would puke from working out so hard, but they would still continue.

I felt like if I could push my physical body to its limits and use my mind to push through, then maybe the same could apply to my anxiety.

If panic attacks were my version of excruciating pain, then I thought I could control them with the same rigorous exercise a Navy SEAL would do as well.

Then, I heard the candidates say, "Pain is weakness leaving the body," and I was sold.

The following day, I asked my father if he thought maybe the Navy SEAL candidates could come to school and give the high school a workout. Mrs. Inwood agreed to it without even hesitating, and I felt excited because now I was going to be strong.

Except there was one issue. I hadn't been eating very much at all, and to complete a Navy SEAL workout, you need fuel to sustain yourself.

There I was, lined up with my fellow classmates, attempting

to do push-ups (in which my elbows could barely get to forty-five degrees, nevermind the ninety degrees they're supposed to be at), and all of a sudden, I felt the most extreme nausea and dizziness ever take over my body.

One more set of jumping jacks and I was pretty sure I would die right there on the gym floor, in the middle of a Navy SEAL-style workout.

The sneaky, anxious, brilliant Tessa came up with a plan: ask to go get my water and never come back.

So I went and hid in the nurse's office.

I am free.

Or so I thought.

Then I realized that the candidates were driving me home from school.

Damnit, my father thought this would be cool, but now it just honestly sucks.

Maybe I can hide in here for the night? My anxious mind searched for possible escape routes from the candidates, but before I could come up with anything good, they found me in the nurse's office.

Great.

Needless to say, they drove me home and I didn't die of embarrassment, but in fact, one of the candidates offered to give me workouts in return for my dad teaching him about energy medicine.

This is how I became a badass fourteen-year-old. I started to do Navy SEAL workouts and train like I was fighting for my life (or the sanity of my mind).

I became fascinated by how the human body converts food into energy. It all just seemed so cool (and slightly magical!). After working out with the Navy SEAL candidate, I realized I had to get my shit together in the eating department. Starving myself for 36-48 hours was no longer going to work if I wanted to be a beast at burpees. Starving myself to be thin was no longer an option.

Out of pure motivation to be physically stronger, I decided I needed to eat. Even if mentally it seemed like I was making myself "fat" at first, I wanted to be strong, and deep down, I knew eating properly was the key.

But I had absolutely no idea what I was doing.

Kale? Almond milk? Salmon? I had never eaten those things before, and now I was making sure we had it all in the house.

I became a mad scientist in the kitchen. I found the freedom to experiment was just an absolute joy.

Becoming a healthy eater and chef was a huge lesson in being okay with failure.

Sometimes I'd cook something that was absolutely horrible. This was usually when I was attempting to cook salmon (even though I generally dislike fish). I'd often burn it or get a mini anxiety attack over the skin of the salmon. But soon, I'd start to laugh because however this fish that I despised turned out, it was funny.

The journey of health was no longer intimidating because I could laugh and have fun at my mistakes. My almost burning down the kitchen moments. My forgetting to put the lid on the blender moments. My attempts at juice cleansing gone bad moments. It was all these little fun oh-no's that ultimately led to a great sense of humor about life.

Then, when the kale smoothie turned out oh-so-delicious, and the homemade protein bars turned out to be a staple in my home, I felt so accomplished.

It made me want to scream, "I AM F***ING AWESOME, WORLD!"

I don't think I fell in love with health because of its tastes or how my body looked as a result. I fell in love with health because it was a constant journey of adventure, fun, and feeling fantastic.

Those are the reasons one should fall in love with health. It's no longer about looking good or keeping a green juice like an accessory these days. It's all about failing, learning, growing, and taking that vibrancy out into the world.

In the same year, I took a yoga class with a bunch of moms. I was clearly the youngest by about twenty or thirty years.

All of the other women in the class always requested to have extra meditation time, except me.

During the savasana/meditation time, I did anything but meditate. I replayed the entire day in my head (you know, specifically obsessing over the parts of the day that caused anxiety), or I obsessed over everything that had to be done after yoga.

These are some of the thoughts that would replay rather loudly in my mind:

You sounded like an idiot when you asked that question in algebra today. Now everyone thinks you're a stupid failure.... wait, breathe. Just Breathe.... I can't because I am a stupid failure. Stupid Failure. The most stupidest of failures of all time who can't do algebra!

It's thoughts like these that would leave my mind racing. By the time the yoga class was over, I actually felt more stressed from all the nervous, angry thoughts I had during savasana.

The following year, the Universe thought I was in a place that needed some meditation in my life. So, the magical powers of the Universe brought me Miss Casey.

During the summer, I spent time at my school getting my summer work done alongside my trusted bodyguard, Nathan. One hot summer day, Nathan decided to take me down into the new wing of the high school where we met Miss Casey for the first time.

My immediate thought was, "Oh, no. I am going to fail her class."

Yup, failing a meditation class. That's where my mind went!

I looked at Miss Casey with fear in my eyes. Pure raging fear.

When I really looked at Miss Casey, though, the fear shifted. I saw this grounded, smiling woman who once lived with anxiety. If this thing she calls "mindfulness" helped her get there then, by all means, I guess I have to try it.

When she explained to me that mindfulness was simply watching your thoughts without judgement, I knew I had to try it. Before then, all I had known was judgement, so the opportunity to WATCH thoughts WITHOUT judgement seemed like just the perfect thing for me.

See, the Universe, God, whatever you believe in, really does present you with what you need exactly when you need it because you can handle it. But that awareness didn't just happen overnight.

With the addition of Miss Casey, along came a week-long mindfulness endeavor that Mr. Quirk thought would be beneficial.

I liked Mr. Quirk. I really did. But I thought he was mad wacky for kicking off his role as the director of the high school with mindfulness. Who thinks that might be a good idea?

I had no choice but to roll with it. I liked Miss Casey, but I thought she was also mad wacky for believing this stuff actually worked.

So I sat with my entire high school of about twenty kids and we practiced mindfulness.

Whatever that meant.

Miss Casey had this singing bowl and when she would tap the bowl, we'd close our eyes and try to listen to the sound as long as it lasted.

Real fun, Mr. Quirk.

I tried to do this mindfulness thing, but my mind was full, and trying to calm my racing thoughts felt damn near impossible. So I resisted it.

I'd think about the list of reasons I was going to tell Mr. Quirk he should never again start the school year off with mindfulness.

After rebelling against practicing the mindfulness exercises for days in a row, I gave into them. I actually tried to listen to the singing bowl. I tried to watch my breath. I gave it my best. And you know what? I liked it.

It reminded me of my experience in the rain where I could be present in the world and not just stuck in my head. What a relief it was to feel like a human being, actually being!

So instead of making a list of reasons for Mr. Quirk to not continue mindfulness, I asked for a mindfulness class.

I wanted to feel present more often. I wanted to be able to do it on my own. I wanted to learn from Miss Casey. But the neat thing was, I wasn't the only one.

Other students in my school wanted to experience mindfulness as well because they, too, had finally felt what it was like to be present. It was such a gift to high school students who rarely *weren't* worrying about the past or obsessing on how to get on to the future. A few of us were able to understand that and we absolutely loved that we were able to get a class period to experience this new feeling.

I then began to notice when anxiety was starting to creep up on me, and instead of worrying about the anxiety turning into an anxiety attack, I just noticed it. I could find the root of the panic without even having to panic.

This didn't happen all at once. I didn't wake up with a mindfulness epiphany.

Mindfulness is like a muscle. In order to strengthen being mindful in the face of anxiety, I had to actually practice it.

But that wasn't always easy.

My anxiety didn't want to go away. It was going to put up a good fight, but I had to get so tired of the anxiety voice and the terror it wreaked on my mind and body to want to strengthen the mindfulness muscle.

Mindfulness taught me that anxiety is a choice. I can choose to partake in the anxious voice and welcome the thoughts into my mind. Or, I can say, "No, thanks."

It wasn't easy to say no to my anxious voice. I had been living with it all of my life. It's all I'd ever known. But by going to therapy and talking about my anxiety aloud with my therapist, Todd, I began to hear how crazy the anxiety sounded.

Let's be real: The chances of me being hit by a plane falling out of the sky are slim to none. But anxiety had me believe there was a 100% chance that I was going to be that ONE person who would get hit by a plane for standing outside.

When I heard these thoughts aloud in therapy, I could discern on my own what was anxiety and what was Tessa's voice.

Because guess what? ANXIETY IS NOT TESSA. NOT ONE BIT.

Woah. Now that was an epiphany!

I learned to hear the anxious voice. Its phrases would usually start with, "What if...?" or, "You are going to..."

Once those phrases would begin, I noticed them and let them pass without following along down the rabbit hole.

Don't get me wrong. It wasn't every time that those phrases appeared that I stopped myself from going down the rabbit hole. There were many times that I would follow the phrases and wind up in a panic attack.

As much as I wanted to get totally angry with myself for going down the rabbit hole and "giving into" anxiety, I chose to forgive myself. I honored that I was learning and that no one gets it perfect on the first try. Heck, no one gets it perfect on the hundredth or the thousandth try! But that's the beauty of it—we have the opportunity to try and try again.

Mindfulness wasn't an epiphany I experienced. It wasn't always easy to implement the practice. But it helped me to build a better relationship with myself by practicing the art of forgiveness.

Watching my thoughts without judgement was hard because I was so used to judging myself. But living with a constant anxiety voice was harder. I chose to practice mindfulness not because it was easy, but because it was worth it for the sake of my sanity and my life.

I could then apply mindfulness to anything, even my eating habits. Instead of approaching food from an obsessive-manic approach, I used mindfulness to learn how foods made me feel. I stopped categorizing foods based on some blog I read off a sketchy health website (because that was my previous practice of discerning healthy vs. unhealthy).

Applying mindfulness to my eating habits opened up a whole new relationship with my body. I learned to trust myself. It opened my eyes to the fact that I ultimately know what's best for my body if I listen to how it feels and not what my mind thinks.

I could have read a million blog posts on why gluten is bad for you, but I had to experience what gluten I could take and not take. That's also what made me stick to healthy eating habits—I knew how I wanted to feel and what foods allowed me to feel good. Because who wants to feel crappy? I certainly did not.

I fell in love with kale not because it tastes great (let's be real, the first bite of kale is a rough one), but I kept eating kale because I felt like I could do anything after a few bites. My energy felt high and my ability to focus turned on.

One could say mindfulness changed my life, but it was me who changed my life because I implemented mindfulness. Not the other way around.

It took an immense amount of courage to try something new (and a bit funky) like mindfulness, but I ultimately made the decision to continue to try (and sometimes fail) at watching my thoughts and eating habits without judgement.

In your home, you know exactly where everything is. You know at what times your house is busy, and the times it's normally quiet. You know the exact step on the staircase that squeaks. The practice of mindfulness helped me know the home that is my body.

THE WELLNESS TOOLS

I think everyone has a right to not only feel well, but to be well. This doesn't take much thought. Just implementing these simple bits will help increase the wellness in your life. This is about eating good foods, thinking good thoughts, and moving your body in a way that feels good to you. Wellness is not meant to be complicated, but to complement your lifestyle in a healthful manner. These tools really complement the basic foundational tools so you might feel like trying them together. Let's bring on the wellness tools!

Your toolbox needs some wellness tools, so make sure to add which ones fit you best on page 169.

#13 Lesson
THE SECRET TO HEALTH...

...is a well-stocked fridge and pantry. I am not saying you have to have the entire grocery store in your kitchen, but I find that it's easier to maintain a healthy lifestyle when you have versatile foods that are easy to prepare. These are my top twenty must-haves for a well-stocked kitchen (but also note that I am gluten-free, thus the gluten-free add-ins):

1. Frozen bananas: smoothies, "nice-cream," maybe even covered in dark chocolate.

2. Spinach: sautéed, thrown in a smoothie, a simple salad... so many options!

3. Eggs: scrambled, quiche, or for French toast (and a great source of protein).

4. Avocado: God bless avocado toast.

5. Broccoli: protein packed plant (and great to add-in with gluten-free mac & cheese).

6. Unsweetened almond milk: because you're just going to need almond milk during the day.

7. Gluten-free bread or local bakery bread: because yes, we need bread in our lives, especially for avocado toast. If you're going to eat bread, get a stinkin' good quality bread, like rye or sourdough (ideally from a bakery).

8. Peanut butter: the classic addition to a smoothie or partnered with an apple.

9. Quinoa: the staple in all my lunches.

10. Dark chocolate: every gal's favorite in her kitchen.

11. Fresh or frozen berries: hello, smoothie or just a simple sweet treat.

12. Lemon: warm lemon water is a great way to start the day. Also, lemon and olive oil is the perfect salad dressing.

13. Garlic: you may not have friends after eating garlic and smelling your breath, but you will have your health!

14. Apples: one of my favorite snacks.

15. Bean-based pasta: because who doesn't want a bowl of pasta sometimes? Trader Joes has it!

16. Kale: the peanut butter to my jelly, my first green love. Hello, kale chips with garlic!

17. Sweet potatoes: the tastiest potato.

18. Cinnamon: throw in a smoothie, top on your sweet potatoes, or on French toast!

19. Peppers: just because they are oh-so-delicious with eggs and avocado.

20. Olive oil: the necessity in everyone's kitchen.

#14 Tool
BURPEES

Burpees have a negative rap. A lot of people simply don't like them, but for some reason, I love them! They make me feel strong and energized. It doesn't seem like torture to me if the end result is feeling like a beast. For those who have never done a burpee, here's the breakdown:

1. Squat down and place your hands on the floor, just in front of your feet.

2. Jump both feet back at once to land in a plank position.

3. Complete one push-up (you can always drop to your knees to make it easier).

4. Push up back to the plank position.

5. Jump your feet back between your hands.

6. Then finish with an explosive jump.

Burpees are challenging, there's no lie in that. When I first started doing burpees, I could barely do a push-up and I would quickly run out of breath. The key is to start where you are and not give up because this is new for you. Maybe each day add two, three, five, or even ten burpees to your workout. With patience will come results that will leave you proud.

#15 Recipe
SPINACH PANCAKES

Pancakes. The Universe's gift to an awesome breakfast. But hey, usually pancakes leave us feeling like absolute crap. I wanted the pancake without the crap feeling afterward, so I had fun, got playful in the kitchen, and discovered spinach pancakes.

Ingredients:

1 banana

2 eggs

1 handful of spinach

¼ cup oat flour

Dash of almond milk

Coconut oil

Maple syrup

Fresh berries

Instructions:

1. Blend the banana, eggs, spinach, and almond milk together until you have a batter consistency.

2. Meanwhile, heat pan and cover the surface of the pan with coconut oil (about a teaspoon).

3. Once the coconut is melted and has covered the pan, on medium heat, pour batter onto surface.

4. When bubbles start to form, flip pancake.

5. Repeat this process for second pancake.

6. Enjoy with maple syrup and some fresh berries.

#16 Tool
GRATITUDE JOURNALING

When we take the time to notice the little things we're grateful for, the so-called "big things," like anxiety, tests, negative social situations, or depression, start to fade away because they don't seem so big anymore. The little things, like the sun providing warmth for the earth and making your day just a bit brighter— that's big! It's incredible that we have a planet in the Universe that is responsible for keeping us warm. That's something to be grateful for.

I challenge you to start your day off by writing what you're grateful for down every single day for at least one week. Before you even leave your bed, you can already be having a great day because you journaled and wrote it down.

FOUR

....

PASSION

I decided that the summer of my sophomore year should be spent getting over the fear of germs, disorganization, and dirt, so I worked in a preschool.

I was assigned to be an assistant teacher in the three-year-old room.

I knew nothing about three-year-olds.

After the first day, I realized that I wasn't going to be teaching these three-year-olds. In fact, it was the three-year-olds that were going to be teaching me.

My first lesson in the school of being three was all that matters is the now. My threes did not obsess over if they didn't like their breakfast or if a sibling was bothering them. Maybe they did in the moment, but once they became present in the classroom, they were good to go.

Second lesson taught by the three-year-old masters? Forgiveness. I watched them, time and time again, get upset over someone taking their toy or using their crayon, but once the issue was intervened, they'd forgive. They would hug it out and go on to play with whoever they had the issue with. This fascinated me.

But the three-year-olds had no reason not to forgive. If they continued to be upset, they wouldn't be rewarded, and it was play time wasted. Yes, they would cry and complain to me or the teacher, but eventually, they'd forgive. It's not something they would hold onto for the rest of the day, week, month, or year.

The third lesson I gained from my favorite teachers was that having fun was the only option. They simply did not do anything unless it was fun. Every action they did had to be fun. Lunch was fun. Bathroom time was fun. Learning to write their name was fun. Searching for bugs in the grass was fun.

That summer, working with the three-year-olds was probably one of the most joy-filled summers I've ever had because everything was so much fun.

I had a huge thing with germs at the time. I had been struggling with being dirty, but God or the Universe gave me just what I needed—the threes.

I was being sneezed on, dealing with accidents, and what came to be my favorite time with them, searching for bugs.

The hunt for bugs was a fantastic journey for three-year-olds because even if you caught an ant, it was still a huge deal. Every time I found an ant, I'd be surrounded by bundles of love. Hugs and screams of, "Yay, Miss Tessa caught a bug," made the dirt under my nails and the touch of a slug worth it. Seeing their faces light up like fireflies when I put the bug in one of their hands was purely priceless. Then, we'd create a habitat for the bugs to live in in our room. The dirt and germs didn't matter if it meant that the threes had smiles on their faces.

I found a new sense of confidence in my ability to handle bugs and to teach three-year-olds, and somehow, along the way, discovered my inner sass, which had a big mouth.

In the new school year, my high school director, Mr. Quirk, declared that he would be starting a blog. I responded in a rather sassy manner stating, "I can have a better blog than you."

The pure love of being competitive (and maybe a tad of perfectionism) often makes me say and commit to some stupid things. I so dearly wanted to have a better blog than Mr. Quirk, but I had no idea as to what that blog might actually be.

Then it came to me. A blog to inspire young people to be healthy for the sake of maintaining sanity.

I called it *TeenSanity*.

As Mr. Quirk set up his blog, I created *TeenSanity: A Teenager's Guide to Health and Wellness*. But what would I blog about? Sure, I knew about health and wellness, but I had NEVER written anything. I was FIFTEEN years old and hadn't received any sort of formal education in health. All that I had learned had been self-taught, so who was I to offer wellness advice?

But in that moment of doubt, I realized that absolutely no other teen at the time (or no other teen that I knew of) was talking about health in a manner that appealed to teens.

We'd all been lectured about what to eat and what not to eat. No teenager wanted to hear that again.

We all knew that exercise was important, but gym class never motivated us to be active in any sort of way.

So, how could I be successful and beat Quirk in awesomeness?

All of the above was true, but it didn't mean that teens weren't interested in having clear skin, fit bodies, and a glowing demeanor. Every teen wants that. So I thought the blog would have to have some success...and it did.

Then, a new idea was brought to life from that simple teen health blog. I found myself finding my purpose.

It started with my friends asking me how I toned my body and about different exercises for your arms in the hallway at school. I noticed that my friends had absolutely no idea about what it took to be healthy. That's exactly why I'd started *TeenSanity*. But there was something missing.

Why was it that I was thriving when my peers were struggling with anxiety over tests and stressing about pretty much everything? I was the one with the anxiety disorder. I was the one who was supposed to be panicking and stressing out over every little detail.

I looked at my peers and felt sad.

They were de-stressing by seeking out relationships, and rather unhealthy relationships at that. It was all about hooking up with cute guys to escape feelings of loneliness and the overwhelming world of being a teenager. Cigarettes and marijuana were breaks from reality, especially the reality of school and the pressure that came with it. Tubs of ice cream were the cure for when those relationships went sour. Then there was the addition of Facebook and Tumblr, which made it even easier to escape reality, stalk people, and obsess over body image.

Teens wanted to know why they walked around feeling like shit and it was pretty obvious. Eating crap all day, negative thoughts on repeat, and the lack of resources available is a recipe for disaster.

As I poured my heart and soul into *TeenSanity,* I realized that wasn't enough.

Yes, it was great that the now sixteen-year-old Tessa was sharing tips with her fellow peers, but could I really change the outcome for teenagers? Would a blog supply the resources they needed?

It seemed like there was a bigger problem. Schools weren't supplying alternatives for students to gain social and emotional tools. It just wasn't there. I could look back on my middle school years and see that the most frequent form of support that was offered to me was a stress ball.

"Squeeze this ball and all your problems will go away."

For a while, that was the only way I knew how to cope. The stress ball.

I reflected on the fact that I was the lucky one. Not everyone got the full scholarship per year to attend a private school that did supply resources and coping mechanisms for stress, even down to having a mindfulness teacher on staff. If those resources hadn't been in my face at school, it was clear to me that I wouldn't have come to thrive. It was very possible that I could've turned to drugs, alcohol, or relationships to get me through high school and help me to escape the reality of my anxiety.

The audacious sixteen-year-old in me had an idea. The idea was to go into schools as a third party and provide resources and coping mechanisms that would enable teens to thrive. What would the world look like if high schoolers practiced meditation in school? Would we have less school shootings? I believe so.

But what could a sixteen-year-old really do? I was still in high school and everyone just thought I was cute for having ideas.

"Oh, it's so cute that Tessa wants to share her story and help others!"

Cute. Cute. Cute.

I thought I was this RADICAL teenager who wanted to change education by teaching awareness, self-efficacy, the science of happiness, exploration, and tools. I called it ASSET, and three years later, it turned into a non-profit organization called ASSET Education.

What started as an observation later evolved into my passion of solving a desperate need in this world, and I wanted to share it with the world, or maybe just Kris Carr, the woman behind the *Crazy Sexy Cancer* revolution.

At seventeen years old, there was no one I admired more than Kris Carr. Yes, most people at my age were obsessing over what celebrities were posting on Facebook or Twitter. I was obsessed with what Kris Carr ate for lunch.

Clearly at this point, I was a certified health nerd.

Kris Carr was coming out with her *Crazy Sexy Cookbook* (which I highly recommend to all vegans and non-vegans), and it seemed like the perfect time to interview her on my new and improved blog, iamtessa.com.

There was nothing more that I wanted than to talk all things kale and almond milk with Kris. She had taken the pain of battling cancer and used her personal experience to benefit others. Kris reaffirmed for me that just because negative situations are put in front of us, that does not mean we have to stop living our lives, nor should we.

So I emailed Kris's peeps one November afternoon asking if I could interview Kris Carr.

And they said, "No," that she was currently too busy for an interview, but maybe after the book tour she might be available.

Damnit.

I was so upset. I knew Kris's story and outlook on health was so needed to be heard by the teen population. We needed to learn about kale, spinach, juicing, the dirty dozen, for God's sake, the teen world so needed a Kris Carr smackdown!

I felt deep within my dramatic adolescent soul that I was the one who needed to share the Kris Carr wisdom with the teen world.

I searched for my moment of opportunity. How could I get to Kris? Then, the opportunity came when I saw that she would be speaking at a Hay House event in New York City.

Mrs. Inwood and I bought the most expensive tickets available to sit alongside the authors. Without a doubt, the best way to spend my hard earned babysitting money was on the chance to meet Kris Carr. ***Teens who are reading this: Save your money for opportunities that will result in the most personal growth.***

The Saturday morning arrived for the Hay House conference and every bone in my body believed that was the day I would meet Kris Carr.

For weeks leading up to the event, I spent every night visualizing what it would look like to meet Kris. What would be my facial expression? What would I say? How would she respond?

The evening of the first day was approaching and I had yet to see Kris Carr. Where was this green juice gal? I watched Wayne Dyer, Gabby Bernstein, and Nick Ortner get up on stage and do their thing (which, of course, was filled with mind-blowing awesomeness), but where was Kris?

Then, my health idol pranced in like a unicorn, ever so gracefully. She took her seat just ten seats away from us! TEN SEATS! I think I had a heart attack in that moment as I almost screamed to the entire audience of over five hundred people that Kris Carr had arrived.

EAGLE HAS LANDED!

Just as she sat down, the next round of talks began. I did not watch the talks. I stalked Kris Carr.

Yes, I am one of those health nerds.

The round of talks ended and I sprang up from my seat. Without looking like a total loon, I darted over to where Kris was sitting.

There was the lady I oh-so-admired; the one who did not let cancer get the best of her; the one who started a revolution out of diagnosis.

God, I wish I could be just half as cool as you someday.

Those were not the first words I said to Kris.

They were actually, "Hey, Kris Carr. I'm seventeen years old. What would it take for me to interview you?"

With a rather confused look on her face, she asked, "What about?"

"Well, I grew up with anxiety disorders and found that health really helped me to thrive. I noticed my fellow teen peers were not doing as well as me and they did not have anxiety disorders. So today, I blog about tools and coping mechanisms that teenagers can use to be healthy. I think your wisdom needs to be shared with the teen world."

Then she said the most beautiful words, "Can you do it tomorrow?"

And in my head, I screamed, *F**K YEAH!*

But in reality, I said, "Yes, of course!"

The rest of the conversation involved how we would meet up at the end of the conference the next day.

I called my mother immediately afterwards, and with all the passion in the world, I announced that, I, the seventeen-year-old anxious teen would be interviewing a New York Times Bestselling author.

There's nothing like achieving what is seemingly impossible. It makes everything you've ever wanted appear to be in your grasp.

That very next day, with a cute outfit, my father's iPhone, and a boatload of joy, Miss Casey and I arrived at the Javits Convention Center, ready to interview Kris Carr.

Task one was done as the previous night my father and I went to the Apple store to get a mic so I could voice record the interview.

Task two was proven to be a lot more difficult as I wanted to get the interview questions to Kris. I had never interviewed anyone before, but I figured it was a kind gesture to prep them beforehand.

This is where I learned an important lesson. If you pretend like you're supposed to be where you are not supposed to be, no one will assume differently. I walked around the lobby searching for someone who worked at Hay House. They redirected me to the PR person who represents all of the authors at the conference.

Oh shit.

This was my brick wall—the PR person. Did she have the

power to stop my interview? But Kris agreed to it!

I went up this PR person and asked how I would get in contact with Kris. I casually explained how I was a blogger who reached out to Kris directly and how she had agreed to be interviewed.

With a rather suspicious look on her face and my eyes wide, she walked me to the green room where, of course, Kris was not there yet, but her questions were!

The day had gone on and I felt truly exhausted. The rush of excitement was wearing off and the reality that I would be interviewing a role model of mine was quickly approaching.

As I waited for Kris to finish signing books, I sat on the floor of the Javits Center with Miss Casey, agreeing that this was the only place we could find to interview her. Kris was surely easy going enough that if a seventeen-year-old asked her to sit on the floor of a major convention center, she might actually do it.

Classy, right?

But the ever graceful, witty Kris Carr moved us into the green room to conduct the interview. As I sat down next to Kris, I thought I might actually explode with gratitude. She was the first person who I truly admired who ever gave me the time of day. Though she was super busy and just finished keynoting a major event as well as signing books for over an hour, she still made time for an interview with a crazy seventeen-year-old.

Then, without an ounce of anxiety (okay, maybe a few ounces), I interviewed Kris Carr. We talked about going ninja on kale and how teens could eat just a bit healthier. I admitted that I might need to enter Kale Anonymous for I had a bit of an addiction to that scary looking vegetable.

The interview lasted less than ten minutes, but to this day, it is still one of the best ten minutes of my life. For it was the ten minutes that I made something out of nothing.

THE PASSION FUEL TOOLS

You've come to the passion fuel tools and they are just that—
some sweet fuel to ignite your inner badass. These tools are for
the moments when you need a reminder of why you are awesome.
Or for the moments when you feel unmotivated to do anything
(maybe it's that paper that's due next Friday!). Or maybe you need
some actual food fuel before you rock out a workout that (slightly)
scares you. That's what this section of the book is for—to help you
unleash and own your full potential in every aspect of your life.

Don't forget what helps make you a badass and write it down!
Take notes! Get crazy building that one-of-a-kind toolbox of
yours... you know, on page 169.

#17 Mantra

I SHIFT MYSELF TO UPLIFT OTHERS.

Throughout our teen years, it is common for us to feel helpless. Sometimes, the world seems like a cruel place that is out to get you. Though this can be hard to face, the most successful way of helping ourselves is to help someone else.

I didn't initially turn to working at a preschool to feel empowered, but to my surprise, confidence in myself and my abilities was the outcome. Now, I am not saying everyone who reads this book should go work at a preschool to find a sense of empowerment. But I do believe everyone who reads this book should find time, a place, and people they can be of service to.

Whether it's working for an NGO or volunteering at a senior center, make sure you get a daily, weekly, or monthly dose of service in. Trust me, you'll be surprised at how you feel when you give yourself to be of help to others.

#18 Recipe
HOMEMADE VEGAN BROWNIE PROTEIN BARS

I mean, who doesn't love brownies? Gooey chocolate in a protein bar... ummm, yum!

TeenSanity was all about simple ways teens could remain sane in high school. One of the simplest tricks I often shared was about keeping blood sugar stable. It's pretty simple, my friends, but when our blood sugar gets too low we become irritable and rather cranky. This happens when we skip meals (yes, I am talking to you boys and girls who think it's okay to skip breakfast). Then there's the issue of when our blood sugar spikes and then crashes. Ever face dive into a pizza or a bunch of sugary sweets and thirty minutes later you feel like crap? Like you actually just consumed the gross feeling? You can thank the rise and crash of your blood sugar for that one.

So these brownie protein bars, huh? These are my go-to snacks for anyone. When I make one batch, within less than forty-eight hours, my entire family and I devour them.

Ingredients:
1 can black beans (drained and rinsed)
½ cup peanut butter
¼ cup applesauce

¼ cup agave nectar

1 tsp. vanilla extract

½ cup Sunwarrior Warrior Protein Blend

½ cup raw cacao powder

½ cup dark chocolate chips

¼ cup sliced almonds

¼ cup raisins

1.5 cups oats

Coconut oil

Almond milk

Instructions:

1.   Preheat the oven to 350°F.

2.   Using a food processor or blender, combine black beans, peanut butter, applesauce, agave nectar, and vanilla extract until smooth.

3.   Next, add the oats, raw cacao powder, and protein powder and combine into mixture.

4.   Add the dark chocolate chips, sliced almonds, and raisins and pulse to combine. If it's too dry and you're struggling to combine the ingredients, add in almond milk as needed.

5.   With a baking pan, coat the pan with coconut oil and evenly spread mixture as if you were baking brownies. Then bake at 350°F for 15-20 minutes. You should be able to stick a fork in the protein bars and have it come out clean.

#19 Tool
EMOTIONAL FREEDOM TECHNIQUE

I was first introduced to EFT, or Emotional Freedom Technique, by my mindfulness teacher, Miss Casey. But as the typical teen, I thought tapping different acupressure points on your body was rather strange and couldn't possibly be of benefit to me.

A year later, a book called *The Tapping Solution* by Nick Ortner came out and simply blew up my Facebook newsfeed. Every health role model I admired was talking about EFT and how it significantly helped them with so many issues, from changing eating habits to back pain to even anxiety.

If that wasn't enough to intrigue me, when the Sandy Hook shooting happened just a few towns from mine, a woman by the name of Lori Leydon was brought to Connecticut to run the Tapping Solution Foundation to help survivors. My father met Lori and became friends with her. He then shared with me her work with the survivors of the Rwandan Genocide. The Universe kept sending me messages that I needed to start using EFT. Once I did, it became clear as to why.

EFT was a tool that I always had with me. I could not make up any excuse as to why I couldn't practice EFT. I started to use it before I went on dates when anxiety arrived. I'd sit in my car and start tapping while venting all of my anxious thoughts about how my date could go potentially wrong. I started practicing in the bathroom at school before tests if I didn't want anyone to see me looking like a crazy lady.

How it works:

I am not an EFT practitioner, just an avid user of the technique.

The first thing I do when practicing EFT is close my eyes and meditate on what it is that is producing the anxiety or high levels of stress. I "tap" into how it is that I am feeling right in that very moment. I then rate how intense the emotion is on a scale of 1 to 10. Maybe I am about to take an algebra test and I know algebra is a trigger for panic attacks, so I'd rate my anxiety at like an 8.5. I feel as if I am about to explode, but I am not exploding yet.

Then, I go on to tap the pinky finger side of my hand with the pointer, middle, and ring finger of my other hand as I say (out loud):

"Even though my anxiety is at an all-time high, I love and accept myself."

"Even though I am extremely worried about this algebra test, I love and accept myself."

"Even though math produces a lot of anxiety for me, I love and accept myself."

Then, using those same three fingers, I go on to tap other parts of my body and vent. Yes, you get to vent! This is one of the reasons why I think EFT is so freaking cool.

As I tap slightly above my eyebrow three to five times, I say, "This anxiety..."

Then, I tap the side of the eye three to five times, "feels like it's killing me..."

Now tap under the eye three to five times, "I feel paralyzed on tests..."

Next, tap under your nostrils and above your lips three to five times, "This anxiety...."

Now tap below your lips and above your chin three to five times, "makes me feel like a loser..."

Tapping the collarbone three to five times, "Anxiety sucks..."

Then, tapping underneath your armpit on the side (if you're a female, under your armpit where your bra is), "I feel frustrated with myself."

And ending on the top of your head, tapping, "This anxiety."

Take a moment to feel what it's like to be you again. Maybe you notice your shoulders aren't touching your ears and your jaw isn't clenching anymore. Rate where your anxiety or whatever emotion/pain you were tapping on is at now.

You can continue to tap as long as you need to feel a sense of relief.

I find that a couple of rounds can really help me realign with a calmer Tessa, and it helps me to leave the obsessive, anxious, slightly looney girl behind.

#20 Lesson
SEEK INSPIRATION

I knew I would find it hard to introduce a social-emotional curriculum into the education system while pursuing a degree in social entrepreneurship.

Challenges would arise. Brick walls would be there. So I needed an unwavering source of inspiration.

I found that when the doors to opportunities closed, I could reflect and say to myself, "Remember, this is not about you. This work is for all the students who are standing in the shoes you were in just a few years ago."

When I reminded myself of the potential impact that a social-emotional curriculum could have on students, the challenges didn't seem so difficult.

Sometimes, it's hard to push through rough situations for ourselves. It's easy to give up and say, "Oh, it's just me. I'll let it go." But when you identify some other reason for why you're pushing through anxiety, battling depression, or building an idea, this reason will help get you through the hard parts.

There will be times when it's easier to hide in your bed and escape the world.

I've found that your source of inspiration has to be

connected to love. You have to have an unwavering love for your inspiration.

When that love is there, connected to your inspiration, it'll make all the difference. It will get you out of bed, ready to conquer the brick walls in your life.

#21 Recipe
KRIS CARR INSPIRED GREEN SMOOTHIE

I'll be honest. I have a sweet tooth. I find it hard to live in a world of gluten-free/dairy-free treats loaded with sugar. I crave those yummy cookies and cupcakes with those pretty "gf" labels. Living in Boulder, these treats are easy to find.

So, one must conquer the world of sweets with nutrient-rich smoothies. There's nothing I love more than greens blended with chocolate. I know this may seem scary, but trust me, chocolate and avocado is a heavenly combination.

This smoothie is inspired by the one and only Kris Carr for its greenness, chocolate goodness, and all around abundant healthy qualities.

This may be chocolate heaven and my favorite way to start the day. Because, as Tara Stiles, yoga rebel and badass would say, "Who made the rules?"

There aren't any rules against having a chocolate smoothie for breakfast in my rulebook. So bliss out!

Ingredients:

½ avocado

1 handful spinach

1 cup almond milk

1 tbsp. peanut butter

2 tbsp. raw cacao powder

1 date (pitted)

Instructions:

1.   Put all dry ingredients in blender, then add liquid.

2.   Blend until smooth.

#22 Lesson
START A PIGGY BANK FOR PERSONAL GROWTH

Maybe it doesn't have to be a piggy bank, but please, just SAVE YOUR MONEY, TEENS.

The point of this lesson is that you should allocate your money to things that will help you to grow. This could be a medical conference because you really want to become a doctor. Find a way to get to that conference, because who knows where it may take you. Maybe you'll even learn you don't want to be a doctor after all. But guess what? That's OKAY. In fact, it's better than okay, it's growth because you uncovered a layer of yourself.

When I saved my babysitting money, I had no idea I was going to put it towards a Hay House conference to meet Kris Carr and interview her.

But the awesome part was when the opportunity appeared, I was able to take ahold of it.

If I hadn't saved my money, I still would have tried to go by emailing Hay House with my story, trying to get a press badge, or some other scheme. So here's the other thing: If an opportunity arises and you still cannot afford it, find a way. Even if you ultimately are unable to take ahold of the opportunity, I promise the efforts of finding another way will be just as great. Use the student card. Works every time.

When we make attempts to go after the things we so desperately want, we grow, we learn something new about ourselves. That's priceless because you can take your own growth anywhere and it will benefit you in ways you could not possibly imagine.

What is this growth she speaks of?

It doesn't have to be this complicated, over-used word.

In my opinion, it's the moment you choose to step outside of your comfort zone, even if it's taking two steps into a health food store and leaving (that's growth because you took those two steps!). Do not underestimate the power of a single step. Growth can come in the form of asking your teacher for help with a college application because you have absolutely no clue what to put down. Asking for help is growth because it furthers you along, gets you closer to whatever you want to achieve.

Now, this book was not written to be some self-help book, but here it is peeps: Go grow yourself and save your money so you can.

That's it.

FIVE

....

FINALLY FINDING PEACE

There were very few people who thought I'd graduate high school. Because, let's face it, for a while, I could barely enter the school building. As the final months of my senior year approached, it became clear that this crazy, anxious lady would indeed graduate high school. So, the new question everyone had in their head was, "What is next for Tessa?"

During my senior year, high school was a comfortable place. I didn't need to take many classes and it was easy to simply float along, enjoying the freedom of a driver's license and entertaining the idea of changing the education system.

But looming over my head was the notion that I'd have to leave high school, and typically, that meant going off to college. There was this pain in my chest with the thought of going off to college. I knew I'd have to take some sort of standardized test and that was not going to happen. (Once I had such a bad panic attack during one of those tests that I freaked out the kid next to me.) So where was my place in this world?

This is a question that every young person faces in their life. The question of, "Where do I belong outside of the world I know; outside of the home I grew up in?"

This is a scary question, and instead of asking ourselves this, we most often align with what we think is the safest bet.

I stuck to my guns that I did not belong in a traditional school and that I needed to be creating a program to teach anxious students how to thrive. I didn't know what this would look like or how it would unfold, but I knew that settling for anything else would be a waste of energy and produce immense anxiety for me.

In April, when my Facebook feed filled up with posts of college acceptances, the opportunity to apply to Watson University popped up for me. A model of education that had never been done before, Watson University was branding itself as the "Olympic-training ground for social entrepreneurs."

With utter stupidity and no sense of how the college process actually works, I had great trust in that the Universe was conspiring this exact opportunity for me all along. I knew I belonged at Watson University, and not only that I belonged there, but Watson needed me just as much as I needed it.

I think my belief that there had to be something more than just going to a traditional university was what ultimately got me to Watson. It's these strong, innate parts of ourselves that we must listen to, because with that listening comes great insight into what we should actually pursue.

By some strange miracle, I got into Watson. I got into college. I was going to move far away from home to the lands of Boulder,

Colorado.

TAKE THAT THERAPIST #5!

Even when one gets into college, there are still senior finals to take.

But I was real sick and tired of school. I wanted to go onto the next thing, the so-called "better thing" called college. I didn't want to take finals and Mr. Quirk knew it.

So he told me to fail my last final, which happened to be my Spanish final.

Yes, my high school director told me to fail a test ON PURPOSE.

I was utterly perplexed.

Why? Why, Quirk, must I fail this final?

I still enjoyed being a perfectionist. Though I knew grades were external representations of happiness, it didn't mean I liked getting good grades any less. I was still a sucker for that A+.

This was a hard choice: To fail or not to fail?

Ultimately, I chose not to fail. Mr. Quirk wasn't disappointed in me.

I realized why he wanted me to fail the Spanish final. His one last lesson for me as a high school student was that I would fail in life. There would be failures. But these failures wouldn't stop me if I didn't let them.

Heck, they could catapult me forward in ways I never could have possibly imagined.

Failure is only failure if one chooses to see it as that. Mr. Quirk was trying to get me to see that.

Then the moment arrived when I would defy all odds and graduate high school.

I'd defy the therapist who told me I would live at home for the rest of my life and never go to college.

I'd defy the middle school psychologist who told my parents the only thing they could do was medicate me and hope that things get better.

I'd defy my inner belief that there was not much to expect from me because I was an anxious soul who wouldn't amount to much.

Yet, there I was, looking in the mirror at the girl who had cried herself to sleep for so many nights and painstakingly worked her butt off to make it through school, even though, day after day, it seemed liked a massive struggle. The struggle was worth it because I sat and looked in the mirror and was proud of who I had become.

My graduation felt like an out-of-body experience. Never in my wildest dreams did I anticipate being able to graduate.

But just as I had started this journey to graduation, I ended it in the exact same way— with Mrs. Inwood right beside me.

I looked at her with gratitude radiating from my bones, and my words to her as graduation began were, "We did it."

"Yes, honey, we did."

So, I sat there, with Mrs. Inwood holding my hand, just the same way we'd started, and with the greatest sense of pride I'd ever felt. Though I sat there holding her hand, it was accepting and welcoming the help of this woman that got me to this point, sitting at my graduation. I no longer feared her help or anyone else's because with help is how I got anywhere on this journey.

It came time for me to speak. I was the last one of our graduating class to give a speech. I read aloud lists of what every teacher at that school had taught me.

Mrs. Inwood taught me that school could be a safe place and anxiety did not have to define my life.

Mr. Quirk taught me to laugh at the ridiculousness that is anxiety and to laugh with all of my heart.

Nathan taught me that I had a backbone, and for the moment when I felt I didn't, he'd be there to be my backbone.

Miss Casey taught me that mindfulness was not something monks did sitting on a mountain, but that mindfulness was a tool to navigate the difficulties of life and to be able to bask in the glory that is life.

I mumbled something that was about what my parents had taught me, but those words could not be expressed in that moment, they could only be felt. I felt unbounded love from them for having not given up on their anxious daughter. By not giving up, I had defied all odds. I graduated high school and was accepted as part of the inaugural class at Watson University.

BAM!

That's how you graduate high school with an anxiety disorder—like an unapologetic, proud as can be badass, owning her gifts as a human being.

The summer of 2013 arrived with bountiful opportunities and great learning lessons before I headed off to college.

I practiced mindfulness in relation to the anxiety I felt in school, but on my first trip by myself, my mindfulness skills were put to the test.

I headed to Chattanooga, Tennessee for a retreat put on by the Thiel Foundation. I felt so honored to be invited to their first ever retreat.

I was sitting on my first flight from New York To Charlotte, North Carolina where I realized that I had forgotten my makeup.

Now, every girl reading this book recognizes how significant it is to forget your makeup when you are on your way to a retreat where you will also be speaking on a panel in front of the Board of Education for that city—big deal. No makeup.

The panic spread everywhere in my body. It was as if venom was taking over my body ever so quickly. I wanted to brainstorm with my parents what I could do, but there I was, stuck on this damn airplane next to a guy snoring his heart out.

One of the biggest fears associated with panic attacks is having them in front of people in unsafe spaces. That fear was seeping through as well.

In this moment, there was only one thing to do:

Stop. Drop. And meditate.

I realized that if I closed my eyes and began to focus on my breath, no one on this plane would know that I was meditating. It would look like I was simply taking a nap.

I never want to stand out when having an anxiety attack, so the immediate choice to fit in amongst the panic was a huge relief.

From there, I transitioned into a mindful state where I participated in my breath. I actively inhaled and exhaled. In engaging with my breath, I was telling my body we could calm down.

After a few minutes of this active engagement in my breath, the venom was no longer there. I realized that, like I had chosen to participate in my breath, I could make the same choice about the venom. I choose not to. Instead, I chose to visualize finding makeup in the airport.

I saw myself walking ever so calmly through the Charlotte airport during my layover to discover a place where I could purchase makeup. In that moment of visualization, I felt what it would feel like to find the makeup—my shade of foundation and a fun lip gloss. Not only was I visualizing the experience, but I was tapping into what it would feel like.

When I walked into the main terminal, I found a store selling makeup in which the same feelings I visualized took over me.

I just laughed because, there I was, having this panic attack at 30,000 feet in the air, then meditating and visualizing, and within an hour, I was able to find the exact place and things I needed.

The Chattanooga plane panic attack seemed fairly insignificant compared to where I found myself a month later when moving to Colorado.

It seemed fitting to drive my stuff to Colorado, but my first car was not going to make the journey. There was a Watson scholar from Massachusetts who wanted to drive his stuff across in his mother's minivan, but his mom would be away during the time he planned to drive.

So, it seemed I had the perfect fit: The mom, the additional stuff, and a driving ability.

But I didn't realize I would be accomplishing more than just moving, I'd be learning about how talented I am at crying.

There are some accomplishments one just has to own for the sheer fact that they're impressive. I have cried through the entire state of Pennsylvania.

That, my friends, is one accomplishment that takes years of practice—the ability to endlessly cry for eight hours with no shortage of tears.

I was in a stranger's car, with my mother at the wheel, driving across the country to Boulder, Colorado, crying the whole way.

The bonus? I'd never visited Boulder or even been to the state of Colorado. But now I was moving there at just barely eighteen years old.

I sat in that moving vehicle for a three-day adventure to await what seemed like the ultimate death of me (because, as we know, most anxiety feels like it might very well be the death of you).

There's one thing I know about anxiety to be true: when it hits you, it does not matter where you are or who you are with. It can be extremely difficult to access that mindful being within or to feed yourself that green smoothie that will for sure calm you down.

I am not going to lie here. It's hard to stop a semi-truck of anxiety from running you over.

Sometimes, it's damn right impossible. Sometimes, we just have to accept that.

Because there I was, the girl who had spent so much time eating well and moving past her brick walls, but now I felt as if I was right back where I'd started. That was the most difficult part of this trip. As every mile passed, I felt like a piece of the strength I had spent the past five years building was farther away from me.

Mrs. Inwood would not be there to meet me at the finish line or to hold my hand, and my mother would not be there to pull back the covers when I didn't want to go to class.

I was no longer going to be able to go to class with Miss Casey and get a dose of mindfulness with my peers.

Mr. Quirk would not be there to motivate me every time I questioned or doubted myself.

It was all on me.

I arrived in Boulder and completely resented the city.

My anxiety and panic attacks were flaring up in every which way and direction. In my opinion, this growth thing now completely sucked.

I was there, in my new environment, just trying to survive, which meant drinking tons of green juice and hiding in my closet.

I spent hours hiding in my closet or under my bed throughout my first few weeks in Boulder. I wish I was kidding, but I am not.

I went to Boulder to change education, but for many weeks, I felt like I couldn't even leave my room. I'd call Miss Casey sobbing or leave Mr. Quirk voicemails with barely any words being spoken, just loud cries and the sound of me sniffing back up the snot.

Pleasant.

I felt incredibly lost in my new world, being at a school for the world's most promising change makers. Trust me, my fellow Watson scholars were some of the most inspiring and resilient people I'd ever met. They weren't battling anxiety, but battling their corrupt home countries, even some having grown up in refugee camps. Yet they were building schools, changing culture, and taking on enormous environmental challenges—but there I was, panicking because I felt like my world had just been turned upside down.

How could I justify my feelings?

I wanted to judge myself and admit that I didn't fit in. But that would be giving in to anxiety once again, and I had lost so many experiences from giving in to anxiety.

I had to try to create a life for myself in Boulder despite all the anxiety. So I'd wander around the city, through the farmer's market, and practice taking note of things I was grateful for about Boulder.

I was grateful to have roommates who didn't question my anxiety and let me have the single room within our apartment.

I was grateful for Eric, the president of Watson, for being my person in Boulder who made sure I went to class and made the most of the experience.

I was grateful to be part of the inaugural class of Watson University, and to be part of a community that was taking action in changing the world.

I was grateful for Boulder's health conscious environment where gluten-free goodies were everywhere.

I found myself in this state of tension, wanting to be mad at Boulder, but realizing that every time I wanted to be mad, it got me nowhere.

Being angry did not make the situation any better.

Putting on the gratitude lens did. It made the world seem a little bit brighter than the darkness under my skin.

I joined a gym with my fellow scholar, Ryan. I made sure to make boatloads of green juice and got the other scholars to join in on the green juice parties. I took hikes by myself and took smiling selfies to remind myself what happiness looks like. I put a smile on my face because the frowns were not serving me.

As much as tears do not serve me, there are times when we need to cry.

It is a healthy right of every human being. We have tear ducts for a reason!

It was a Sunday evening in November and I had been having panic attacks all day. I had no idea why. They were just rolling. It just seemed to be one of those days. You know, one of those days were the emotions are there and you just have to let them have their moment.

But I couldn't understand why. I was attending my classes. I was not crying in my classes because of my anxiety. I even dared to raise my hand every so often.

I was doing somewhat well.

I called my mom, explaining to her how I had been having an incredible amount of anxiety for what felt like no good reason at all.

Then she said, "I didn't want to tell you this over the phone..."

Oh shit. This isn't good.

I listened in shock as she told me Mr. Quirk had been diagnosed with a stage four cancer.

My Mr. Quirk, my other dad, my person... not cool, life. Not cool at all.

The rug had been pulled out from underneath me and I was 1,700 miles away from my home where I felt like I belonged.

I wanted to be with Mr. Quirk, to give him a hug and tell him we were going to kick cancer's butt.

But I knew there was no other place Mr. Quirk would want me to be than going to my new university.

This is when I learned emotions have their place even if they seem unnecessary. That night, I cried like I had never cried before in my life. One of my tribe members was sick. I couldn't imagine what it must have felt like for him to have cancer and the immense amount of strength that it would take to fight.

Then, to top off having a father figure with cancer plus living in a strange new place, a Watson scholar student asked me out.

Just what this anxious person needed—another reason to be anxious.

There is no guidebook for dating with anxiety disorders. There just isn't because it's a total shot in the dark.

He had just sold his first company and I just hadn't done anything like that. How was I supposed to date someone who'd accomplished that while my biggest accomplishment that day was getting out of bed and attending class without crying?

On our first date, I had a panic attack... shocker.

I was in the shower beforehand and it hit me. I just wanted to do what was comfortable a.k.a. drink a kale smoothie and watch a movie. Who needed dating? I was just trying to do this whole living on my own thing. Dating wasn't in my cards.

But he insisted, even if it meant staying in my apartment and drinking kale smoothies.

There are clear moments when I have chosen the uncomfortable path and this was one of them. It was so tempting to say, "I am sick," like I had done time and time before to get out of things when I felt anxious. But I really couldn't this time because he'd see me in class the next day, feeling totally fine. I was in a pickle, anxious and pissed that I had agreed to the date.

But comfort zones are meant to be broken.

One date turned into another and then another, which turned into actually having a boyfriend.

Kale smoothies and movies for the win! Lesson learned: be yourself and those that like who that person is will want to be around you. Why try to fit in when it's way more fun to be your authentic self?

My first semester at Watson was incredibly difficult, but I

chose to keep on smiling and prevailing. By continuing to show up to classes, share my ideas, and not give up on myself, I opened up waves of opportunities within which to flourish.

In pushing my own boundaries, I opened the gate wide open to challenge myself in ways that were previously unfathomable.

Like judging a national Canadian business competition.

Let me repeat myself: Like judging a national Canadian business competition.

When the president of Watson, Eric, allowed for me to do this, there were no words. Because a) I had never judged a business competition before, let alone a national Canadian one, b) this was my first year of undergrad, and c) anxiety disorders, duh.

But there I was, boarding a plane to Canada to judge a competition on behalf of Watson amongst a product manager at Facebook, and I didn't have a panic attack...

....at all during the trip.

Did I feel anxiety? Absolutely. But all new things produce anxiety. It's a choice whether to give in to the anxiety or to embrace the excitement.

I embraced the excitement of sitting amongst a bunch of Canadian business leaders at eighteen years old. I was excited to take what I was learning at Watson and be putting it to use in a new form. I embraced my youth because it gave me a unique perspective.

Anxiety or excitement. My choice was excitement.

Many students cannot make that choice. I know I certainly could not for many years.

The anxiety I felt was always a great reminder that I needed to help other students who were facing the same pain under their skin.

It was this painful sensation that kept me believing that I needed to create a safe space in schools.

So, in my second year at Watson, I found myself pitching the idea of teaching a workshop series that would provide coping mechanisms and skills to anxious high school students.

For some strange reason, the school agreed to let me come in and 40% of the anxious population at that school voluntarily signed up!

WHAT?

I was official now. They even gave me my own mailbox at the school.

You know you're official when you have your own mailbox.

There, I met the students who would teach me what it was like to live with anxiety today, and ultimately, they became some of my greatest teachers.

First thing they taught me not to do was to not do a mindfulness raisin activity on the first day. Because no matter how cool mindfulness is, raisins aren't cool and actually frowned upon by most high schoolers.

Lesson learned.

So I returned the second week, not with raisins, but with connecting activities.

What was it that brought all of us into the room together? I wanted to know why they signed up. I learned that multiple people had been called victims, but didn't deserve that label. I learned that it was much harder to strike up a conversation when no one had given you the opportunity to speak. But that didn't mean that some didn't want to speak or share their experiences. In fact, I found that surface level conversations were not what the group wanted, but actually, they wanted to know each other.

There was one girl who was very quiet and some felt worried that she didn't have too many friends. She didn't speak much to me or to the others, but I knew that didn't mean she didn't want to speak. She had thoughts to share.

After just one hour of connecting during the break, I saw her exchange numbers with another student in the workshop.

I almost cried with joy because I knew this had been a new experience for her and I was so happy to be part of it in some small way.

We had just finished an activity called the Diversity Walk. This activity is when you state something like, "Walk across the line if you identify with X." Then, those that identify with the statement walk across the line to the other side. They are then asked to notice how they feel having stepped across the line.

After completing this activity, one of the girls asked if we could do a tootsie roll group hug. The rest of the students agreed, and with huge smiles on their faces, wrapped me in hugs. We went one-by-one and hugged each and every one in the group.

That was week two, and I knew that all the pain of growing up with anxiety was worth it to help this group of students move past their brick walls.

Just when my students were moving past their brick walls, I was faced with yet another one of my own.

I had always been told, "You are so courageous for facing your anxiety head-on every single day."

Yes, that was true. Living with anxiety had taught me what it meant to be gritty and how to access that courageous part of myself every single day. I had become comfortable in this anxiety courage. I knew what it took to mitigate a panic attack or to recover from one. I knew what foods would help me feel best. I knew what tools I could use at any moment of anxiety arising.

But there came a time when the roadmap was unclear. It was in the face of my father's heart attack, where my courage would truly be tested.

You see movies and hear stories of these awful situations happening to people. You can watch or read them from afar, but not participate. You thank God or the Universe or whatever you believe in for all that you have. But then, that moment comes when you are in that awful situation and you are experiencing that terrible phone call.

I had already experienced that one terrible phone call about Mr. Quirk's cancer diagnosis. I most certainly felt I had met my quota of scary phone calls for the next several years.

I had flown my father out to visit me because I knew he was overwhelmed with work and that he just needed some time away from Connecticut. I knew that he was having kidney stones but I thought that a decrease in stress would help. What I did not anticipate was that he would suffer a heart attack on the returning flight from Denver.

I received a call on my parents' anniversary from my mom with the words, "You are not going to believe this, but your dad suffered a heart attack. He's okay, but he had a massive heart attack, they think." I was in the middle of volunteering for a conference when my world just stopped.

Dad. Heart attack. Dad had a heart attack. Massive.

"I am coming home," I declared it amongst tears and the aching pain in the back of my throat.

At the time, I was in an empty storage space, helping to organize goody bags for the conference while my world felt like it had completely fallen apart. I was thirty minutes walking distance from my apartment and I could not imagine walking back up. I could barely understand where I was—what world was I living in where my father suffers a heart attack?

I called my friend to get a ride back to my apartment and sobbed the words my mother had just told me. The lesson here being that it was okay to ask for help.

Oh, and the other kicker? My father wanted to be transferred to the care of Dr. Oz because he had worked with Mehmet in the operating room years ago and knew he would understand how to go about treating my father's condition.

Dr. Oz. Thee Dr. Oz we all see on television. My dad had one potential contact that could lead us to Oz. Even amongst the tears and shock, I made sure we reached out to that one person.

I learned of my father's heart attack at 7pm, and by 1am I was on a flight from Denver to Charlotte, then another flight from Charlotte to New York.

During these flights, there was no such thing as mindfulness or positive psychology. My brain had no room for that. The same words just kept repeating in my head. Dad. Hospital. Heart attack. I distracted my mind by aimlessly watching movies and trying not to think about what nightmare I was currently living in.

I landed at LaGuardia with an email from the Dr. Oz connection who indeed provided me with the name and number of Oz's assistant at Columbia. It's moments like this when I love being an entrepreneur. You can go without sleep and be in a horrible situation and still make progress toward your goal. In this case, mine was to save my dad's life.

My mother was unable to get me from the airport nor did my parents want anyone to know of my father's situation just yet. So I took a bus and then a train to get home, and after twelve hours of what felt like torture, I met my mother at the train station.

As we drove to the hospital, I felt a complete rush of anxiety—

not my normal anxiety, but a rush of fear that my father's life was at risk and I was going to have to see him in this state. I found my dad going in and out of consciousness, looking so small in his hospital bed.

This smallness that I saw and the fear that I felt only made me want to make things better.

Why is it that when it is someone else, we want to fight for them more than we fight for ourselves? Second lesson I learned from my dad's heart attack: fight for yourself as if it is someone else's life.

I called Dr. Oz's person, and with all the energy of trying not to sob the entire conversation, I explained how my father wanted to be in the care of Oz's team and asked what it would take to make that happen.

Third lesson (rather, something that I relearned), if you ask the phrase, "What would it take to make this happen?" and you show how dedicated you truly are, people will generally do everything in their power to help make that thing happen for you.

I was instructed to get my father's transcripts and disks from the hospital and send them to Oz's office overnight. I felt like a secret agent on a special mission—save my father with the rescue and help of Oz's team.

My first obstacle: His current cardiologist.

I begged him to explain to me what made my father's heart attack so massive, yet he danced around it and just said that my father needed surgery. So, I asked for the transcripts for Dr. Oz and made it seem like my dad and Oz were the best of friends (which is not true, they were simply colleagues who had worked together years ago).

I went around the hospital, making every single department who held the key to my father's complete medical transcript feel special and appreciated. For those who questioned the relationship to Dr. Oz, I would just call up my contact and make sure they heard the message of, "You've reached the office of Dr. Mehmet Oz." Those beautiful words would play and the harsh look on their faces would suddenly stop, their eyes would widen.

Damn right I was going to accomplish my mission of saving my dad's life and getting him the care he deserved. If he did not want surgery, I was going to figure out every which way so that would not happen and he would still be safe.

Around the hospital, I was the crazy nineteen-year-old with the keys to Dr. Oz. Within two hours, I was able to get everything sent over to their office.

Time would tell whether or not my dad actually needed surgery.

The next day, I almost burned the house down. I was making chicken and rushed over to the hospital with my mother and forgot to turn off the oven. We returned home hours later to find our house filled with smoke and massive flies. With a sick, sobbing sister and my poor dogs terrified, I rushed them out of the house to find fly traps (because that's what one must do when they almost burn their home down).

On my way to get the fly traps, I received the call from Dr.

Tamyaka, a colleague of Oz's. I explained to Dr. Tamyaka how badly my father did not want to have surgery and how he is a Doctor of Oriental Medicine. Then, he said the most beautiful words, "I do not know much about oriental medicine, but I do know about the heart and I believe your father does not need surgery." I began to cry with gratitude because I'd found the answer I had been looking for the past two days.

I had been searching for the words that my father could be treated with medication and exercise and his own healing. Then, those words were right in front of me. I did it. I'd found the answers.

Within hours and after a lengthy conversation with our insurance company, my father was transferred to Columbia to be in the care of Dr. Oz's team. Five days after his arrival, he walked out the hospital without having had surgery.

I returned to Colorado from my father's heart attack empty. I had given all of myself to my family and I found myself in a body that was exhausted, drained, and lacked the mental capacity to improve.

It is in my darkest, hardest moments that I experience the most growth, even if it's incredibly difficult.

As much as I love my father, I began to resent him for getting sick and not taking care of himself in the first place. Why did he have to have a heart attack? Why did my family have to go through that? I felt like I couldn't trust God or the Universe for it had presented this horrible obstacle in my life.

How was I supposed to conquer my anxiety and change education when everything can be taken away from you so quickly?

Both of the father figures in my life were sick. There was no getting around that reality.

My program for schools was just about to take off. Schools were listening to my vision for education, even welcoming me into their doors.

I had a boyfriend who adored me.

I had an unlimited yoga membership.

I was piloting my university's degree program.

Life looked pretty perfect to the outside world. Heck, I'd be jealous of myself if I were someone from the outside looking in.

But all of these external things really didn't seem to matter when I knew my loved ones could be taken away from me at any moment.

I was living with REAL anxiety now. I had a legitimate reason to feel anxious for the first time in my life and it left me feeling absolutely confused.

Irrational anxiety was easy to overcome in comparison. But real anxiety, the anxiety of losing a loved one to cancer or a heart attack, was there now. I didn't know how to deal with that. I hadn't become an expert in that.

Take some deep breaths and everything will be okay seemed like absolute bullshit. How was there magic in the breath when one's own body could turn on them in any moment? I felt so angry I wanted to punch my pillows for hours to just to let it out.

As I continued to let my anxious thoughts spiral out of control, the more upset I felt. I chose not to stop them.

I found myself aimlessly watching Netflix for hours on end to escape my world. I wanted to forget the feelings of almost losing someone.

I even tried to do a normal activity like go grocery shopping, but I wound up in a car accident with my best friend's car because I blacked out from lack of sleep.

I was either trying too hard to be normal or letting the anxiety sweep me off my feet into oblivion, hiding under my bed for hours.

Yes, I will admit that I hid under my bed for hours. But that's how scared I felt of the realities of life.

I don't know when I started to pick myself up or even how I participated in everyday life activities, but I did.

I ate kale like it was going out of style just because I knew how good it was for me.

If I couldn't bring myself to meditate (which was pretty often), I went to hot yoga class for some form of movement and sweating meditation.

Amongst all the chatter in my head, I did things that I knew were good for me even when I didn't want to do them.

Sitting around feeling sorry for my loved ones and scared about life was helping no one. It wouldn't cure cancer and it would not stop a future heart attack. So why bother? Once again, I had to get so tired of the chatter and fear in my own head to want to stop it.

Why focus on the possibility of losing loved ones when I have them with me right now?

The months after my father's heart attack made me re-evaluate everything. I mean, EVERYTHING.

It seemed to me that illness was linked to negativity and fear. It may not cause sickness, but it does not help it either.

I brought out the mindfulness once again as if I was some superhero saving my own life. I asked myself the question, "What's not serving me?"

Negative thoughts. Repeating the phrase, "Life is scary," could only get me so far. Life was only a hot mess if I focused on the messy thoughts. I needed to stop looking at the bad things that had happened and start being grateful that I had a tough family that was surely fighting to be alive and well.

Not practicing my tools and taking my own advice. You can't just say it, you have to live it. I could preach about the benefits of mindfulness to high school students till they could not take it any longer, but I'd be an absolute joke if I said things were beneficial and did not actually implement them.

Hiding under my bed. Life is not meant to be lived under a bed. As much as I enjoy being an introvert, it does me no good to stop socializing and be an introvert.

The hardest realization. *Being in a relationship I am not ready for.* I could not love this guy if I didn't deeply love myself. It was a radical wake-up call that I needed to focus on who I was rather than try fitting into the image of a girlfriend for the sake of the title. As much as I stayed true to myself, I also embraced having someone take care of me, but I needed to take care of myself. I couldn't rely on anyone else to be my backbone and safety net.

These realizations didn't happen all at once and they were hard.

Dragging myself to 6am hot yoga with weights was brutal.

Making kale smoothies when I'd rather stick my face into a pint of ice cream was a conscious choice.

Breaking up with the boyfriend I very much cared for was like ripping my heart in two.

But it all had to be done to continue to live a life I loved beyond imagination. It had to be done if I wanted to drive education forward. It had to be done if I wanted to love myself as much as I loved the man I was in a relationship with. It had to be done if I wanted to continue to grow.

Anxiety was, once again, no longer the ruler of the Tessa kingdom. It would not serve my heart attack surviving father, or Mr. Quirk, or any of the students I desired to make an impact on. It would serve nothing. If, at the very least, I couldn't do it for myself, I could do it for others in the hopes that one day I would be strong enough to fight for myself.

Life may not always be easy, but it will always be worth it. Anxiety cannot stop that.

THE PEACE(FUL) TOOLS

These tools are like the icing on the cake. They bring it all together—honoring your body, yourself, and your community. I choose these tools when I am looking for an extra boost. It can be anything from a boost of motivation to a reminder, or simply a recipe that is just what I need to honor my body. I love all of my tools, but many of my favorites can be found in this section of the book.

Who knows, maybe your favorites will also be in this section? If they are, you won't want to forget to acknowledge them in your toolbox.

#23 Lesson
FOLLOW YOUR GIFTS

As I said earlier, it's very easy to do what everyone else is doing. That's not hard. It's easy to do what our parents, the generation before us, did. In fact, it's the safe thing to do.

But what we have to realize is that we are growing up in a generation that does not need to follow the past.

What our world needs of us is to use our gifts, so do what you are awesome at.

This is not the spiritual woo-hoo portion of the book.

This is to acknowledge that when we follow paths that are not our own, that do not feel good to us, anxiety is produced. It may not be produced in an anxiety attack like it is for me, but on some level, something will be off and when you tune within, you'll notice it.

#24 Recipe
CHIA SEED PUDDING

To honor one's gifts, one must honor their body. One of my favorite ways to honor my body is with some chia seed love. Rich in omegas, these superfood seeds are some of my favorite additions to all types of dishes—smoothies, French toast, and even PUDDING.

I am not a huge pudding fan, but this chia pudding makes me feel glowing and fabulous inside and out.

Ingredients:

2 cups coconut milk

1 cup chia seeds

4 dates

2 tsp. maple syrup

1 tsp. vanilla extract

Optional: fresh mango and mint to top

Instructions:

1. Blend dates, coconut milk, maple syrup, and vanilla extract until smooth (or the dates are in tiny pieces).

2. Stir in chia seeds.

3. Store in the fridge overnight.

4. Then the MAGICAL, GLOWING CHIA SEED pudding will be yours in the morning!

5. (Optional) Top with fresh mango and mint!

#25 *Mantra*
THE PAST DOES NOT DICTATE THE FUTURE.

The greatest lesson that came from graduating high school was the fact that just because I had grown up with anxiety did not mean I wouldn't graduate.

This was a hard belief to understand because people told me that having an anxiety disorder meant that I wouldn't amount to much. It seemed, of course, the past would dictate my future because my past consisted of anxiety attacks and hiding in my room.

This mantra has taught me that if you believe the past doesn't predict nor dictate your future, it will not. But if you believe that it does, it can haunt you.

In the moments when you feel you have totally failed and messed up the rest of your life, repeat this mantra, because if you stick to this, I can promise you that, with hard work and belief, your future will change for the better.

The past does not dictate my future.

Ahhhh, doesn't that feel good?

#26 Recipe
MASHED SWEET POTATO(ES)

Now that I live by myself, I don't really make large quantities of anything, so excuse the one serving size of mashed sweet potatoes. But it's sweet potatoes that I love to add to the side of any protein and some greens. It's the ultimate potato in my opinion! Don't even get me started on sweet potato fries. Yum! But working with sweet potatoes is rather fun because you get to play with sweetness.

Here's my one-person serving size of mashed sweet potatoes which are extra vanilla-y, just because I love that vanilla-cinnamon-sweet potato combo.

Ingredients:

1 large-ish sweet potato

3 tbsp. almond milk

1 tsp. vanilla

1 tbsp. maple syrup

1 tsp. coconut oil

Cinnamon, to taste

Instructions:

1. Bake sweet potato at 350°F in the oven for an hour.

2. After an hour, scoop out the sweet potato and start mashing with a fork! Get crazy!

3. Once mashed, add in the almond milk, vanilla, maple syrup, coconut oil, and cinnamon. Mix all that together within the sweet potato, and there you have it—a delicious side dish that doesn't take much effort and that you can take your anger from the day out on!

#27 Tool
VISUALIZATION

Visualization is not like you have insane super powers and can imagine something and there it will appear. In my situation with the 2013 summer makeup crisis, it just happened to work out that way.

My mom introduced me to visualization when I was growing up because she wanted to teach me to not focus on all that could go wrong, but instead practice focusing on all that could go right. I would practice visualization before I had an important test to take. I'd see myself walking into the room, which seat I would choose, which pencil I would use, the grade I would get on the test, but most importantly, I would practice the feeling of confidence.

I learned from a teacher in A Course in Miracles, Gabby Bernstein, that by practicing visualization, you were, in fact, participating in a miracle. The definition of a miracle is a shift in perception, a shift from fear to love. I found that moving from a place of fear to a confident visualization was me creating my own miracle. I fell in love with the concept and ability to create my own miracles.

Time and time again, I found that, in some way, I would create a physical miracle—not just a miracle in how I felt, but a miracle in that the situation I was dreading would turn around and surprise me.

So, when the venom of fear or stress or anxiety begins to creep in, remember that you can choose not to participate in the venom, and actually participate in creating your own miracle.

Stop. Drop. Meditate. Visualize. Make a miracle.

#28 Mantra
I BREATHE THROUGH WHAT IS UNCOMFORTABLE.

In yoga, I often find myself in a pose that might be new to my body and rather uncomfortable. I've found that the yoga teacher will always say something about breathing through these poses that are a little uncomfortable.

I've always wondered why I don't just get out of the pose. Why stay in an uncomfortable pose and focus on my breath when I can escape it all by simply releasing?

I found that if I got out of every pose that was uncomfortable, my yoga practice would not be where it is today. I wouldn't be able to do a headstand if I had backed out when it scared me.

What has kept me able to dive into these moments and poses where my immediate reaction is to escape? I breathe. And then I breathe some more.

Because with my breath, I can move through what is uncomfortable.

#29 Tool

WHICH BUCKET WILL YOU CHOOSE?

I once spoke to a mentor and he asked me, "Tessa, if you could put all your marbles in only one bucket, which would it be? Would it be fear or love? You choose."

During this first semester, I kept playing with different buckets. Sometimes I could put all my marbles into love. I could push through the fear and trust that I was going to be okay. I could shift into the gratitude attitude.

But then there were times where it was much easier to sink back into fear. It was easier to hide in my closet or under the covers of my bed than to actually show up to class and face my peers.

I knew that when I chose to put my marbles in the "love bucket" that I felt a ton better. It was harder to make that choice on a conscious level, but the reward was much greater.

Which bucket will you choose?

#30 Recipe
MAMA'S FRENCH TOAST WITH A TWIST

My mom makes excellent gluten and dairy-free French toast.

My mom is not known for her cooking. (Sorry Mom, had to convey how rare and special your French toast is.)

Let me emphasize how rare and special her French toast is. She only cooks three things extremely well: chicken parm, meatballs, and this French toast.

But being the health-obsessed, slightly looney daughter of hers that I am, I had to add a twist to this breakfast dish.

The twist? CHIA SEEDS.

Yes, my friends, they are making a comeback and it's in this French toast that you will want to eat for days and days and days.

Because who doesn't love a kick ass French toast that doesn't make you feel like crap?

Ingredients:

Two slices gluten-free bread

1 egg

2 tbsp. almond milk

1 tsp. vanilla extract

1 tbsp. chia seeds

½ tsp. cinnamon

Coconut oil (for cooking)

Maple syrup (for drizzling on top)

Fresh berries (for a completely delicious addition)

Instructions:

1. Beat egg with almond milk, vanilla extract, chia seeds, and cinnamon.

2. Dip both sides of the bread in egg mixture, coating evenly.

3. On medium heat, cover the pan with a thin layer of coconut oil.

4. Once pan is warm, place evenly coated bread pieces on the hot surface.

5. Let egg mixture cook on each piece of bread. It will turn look slightly browned, but not burnt, and no longer a liquid.

6. Do the same for the other side.

7. Once both sides are cooked, take out of the pan, and drizzle with maple syrup and load on the fresh berries!

#31 Mantra
I FIGHT FOR MY OWN LIFE AS IF IT WERE SOMEONE ELSE'S.

I tell the story of my father's heart attack because too often we give up on ourselves. Maybe we've always felt anxious so we just don't continue to fight to feel normal. Or maybe we feel stuck in a situation that just seems like one massive trap.

I don't think we should wait until massive heart attacks happen to fight for what we deserve or need. It's when we put a significant amount of effort into ourselves that we are rewarded.

We may not always see this at first, or how or if we'll be rewarded. But if we look at our own life and think about what we would want if it were a loved one, we recognize that we need to fight for what we deserve.

Maybe it's not best to look at it as a fight for it encourages tension, but I believe, at times, it is a fight, and it's something worth fighting for—the right to live a life without anxiety, the right to walk into a school building without fear, the right to a safe space where one can call home.

These are the rights worth fighting for, and when you feel like giving up or the mountain seems too great, imagine if it were a loved one's life. Would you try harder for them?

#32 Tool
DON'T TRY TOO MANY TOOLS

In times of desperation, we'll try anything to save ourselves.

In fact, we'll probably try too many things at once.

We'll cut out gluten, begin a daily mindfulness practice, text everyone who's hurt us in the past month, "Goodbye," and commit to veganism within an hour.

Please stop when the rush to save yourself occurs. Because we end up hurting ourselves by spreading ourselves in so many directions that we actually can't take action on any of those practices that might benefit us.

During my time of massive transition in moving across the country, I wanted to practice every single tool in my toolbox all at once.

But in desperation, I found that focusing on simple things was key.

I stuck to being my breath and drinking greens (wherever I could find them in the journey across the country).

When the pain and fear of the unknown in Boulder surfaced, I returned to my breath. I felt my chest rise and fall. I noticed how my belly inflated and deflated. Then I made sure to keep my blood sugar stable with clean, whole foods.

Did I continue to have panic attacks on the journey? Yes.

Was I scared beyond belief? Yes.

Did I make a fool of myself in front of a stranger who I was expected to go to school with? 100% yes.

But I know it could've been a whole lot worse if I hadn't focused on just those simple tools.

EPILOGUE

I can tell you this: Keep going. Keep doing. Keep believing. Keep being.

My last year of college wasn't easy, but it was worth it. I took all the tools and lessons from this book and put them to work. And guess what? They did just that. They worked.

That program that I tested with a bunch of students grew to be integrated into the #1 high school in Denver. I am now training teachers in the program, ASSET, so they can help their students with anxiety by providing effective tools and coping strategies. ASSET will now be in eleven schools in Denver in the fall of 2016 thanks to a grant from Denver public schools. In 2017, ASSET will grow to New York City.

Mr. Quirk's battle with cancer ended in the middle of my final year of college on December 20th, 2015 and I miss him every day. But his impact on my life remains more alive than ever. Every teacher I train in ASSET makes me believe Mr. Quirk's legacy will only continue in education.

My own dad is alive and well. He hasn't suffered a heart attack since his plane episode and I am making sure that never happens again.

I graduated Summa Cum Laude from Watson University and Lynn University with a Bachelor's of Science in Entrepreneurship in three years. I didn't just go to college. I excelled at it.

I practice Strala yoga on the daily because it rewires my brain and body to do everything with ease, instead of tension and anxiety.

I still make kale smoothies (almost) every day. I practice hot yoga five days a week like the hot yoga junkie that I am. I do burpees when I feel I need a burst of energy. Before I go to bed, I practice mindfulness (or whenever the anxiety starts to rise). I recite gratitudes in my head constantly. I don't hide under my bed when I get anxious or call my mother crying.

I do have panic attacks, but very rarely now. I absolutely do not suffer from them. They don't get the best of me... ever. I don't allow them to.

I am constantly laughing at the anxious thoughts because now I find them ridiculously entertaining. I mean, a giant plane crashing on me for walking out of my house? Can't make that stuff up.

My life could not be more beautiful and abundant. It's not that anxiety is absent, but smiles and laughter are more present.

Despite growing up with anxiety, I am not afraid to take on whatever life has in store because that's the beauty of life—you never know what's around the bend. But I do know with these tools, lessons, and recipes, I can handle whatever it may be.

If some magical fairy could come back and make the anxiety disappear from my childhood, I wouldn't allow it. Anxiety has been the farthest thing from a curse and much closer to a blessing. That's right. I said it. A blessing. Though I won't let it take ahold of me, anxiety has given me purpose.

Anxiety is not something I feel debilitated by, but lifted up from. It reminds me that all of us, every single human being on this planet is facing some obstacle, whether it be big or small. However, as humans, our emotions and experiences are what connects us all. Anxiety has become this sacred connector in my life because I can speak to its truths that most would feel afraid to share, though they so desperately want to acknowledge and validate.

I've found that it's not the difficult experiences or personal challenges that define us, but it's what we do with them. I could have easily let anxiety win and take ahold of my story, my life. It could've called the shots—keeping me home instead of going off to college in Colorado. But I've learned to show up, to rise up, when anxiety presents itself, because it's not the anxiety I should be afraid of. It's the power that I let anxiety have. If I don't give anxiety the power to determine my life's course, then it hasn't won. I have.

I'm on a mission; one of those blood, sweat, and tears missions where I have to make sure teachers can help their students cope with anxiety. There need to be more Mr. Quirks and Mrs. Inwoods in this world, and they are out there, but I believe they haven't been given all the tools to help their students. It's my duty to make sure tools to cope with anxiety and stress is taught in everyday classes. Mindfulness, positive psychology, and the tools in this book also belong in the classroom. In fact, they are too crucial to the success and potential of students to not be present.

If there's one thing I hope every reader takes away from this book, it's that you have a choice in how your story will unfold.

I am Tessa.

This is my story.

And it's only just the beginning.

YOUR OWN TOOLBOX

This portion of the book is dedicated to you crafting your very own toolbox.

Special, eh?

Use this as a way to document which tools resonated best with you, where you can apply them in your own life, and what page they're on. This way, you can keep track of all the wonderful resources you have for yourself.

TOOL	WHAT IT'S BEST FOR	PAGE#

TOOL	WHAT IT'S BEST FOR	PAGE#

TOOL	WHAT IT'S BEST FOR	PAGE#

CPSIA information can be obtained
at www.ICGtesting.com
Printed in the USA
LVOW13s0816090317

526557LV00014B/99/P